CSI: PARANORMAL
Investigating Strange Mysteries

BY JOE NICKELL

INQUIRY PRESS
Amherst, NY

CSI: Paranormal—Investigating Strange Mysteries
©2012 INQUIRY PRESS
The Committee for Skeptical Inquiry (CSI), Inc.
PO Box 703, Amherst, NY 14226-0703
Phone: (716) 636-1425 Fax: (716) 636-1733

Printed in Canada

ISBN-10: 1937998002
ISBN-13: 978-1-937998-00-4

Contents

Introduction

Interest in the so-called "paranormal" continues to be high. And the term "paranormal investigation" is now very popular—if often misunderstood.

"Paranormal investigation" is simply the application of appropriate methodologies to the resolution of so-called paranormal mysteries— that is, those supposedly beyond the range of science and normal human experience. This broad term includes not only the "supernatural" but also reported anomalies like Bigfoot and extraterrestrials, which—if they exist—could be quite natural creatures. Since 1969 I have seriously investigated such claims, and since 1995 I have been apparently the world's only full-time professional paranormal investigator.

This role grew out of some of my earlier personas. In 1969 I rekindled my interest in magic—soon working as a magic pitchman in a carnival, then as stage magician, mentalist, magic clown, and escape artist. During the summers of 1970 to 1972, I was Resident Magician at the Houdini Magical Hall of Fame in Niagara Falls, Ontario. This background has aided me in solving many mysteries. I began to investigate paranormal claims in 1969, when I sat in my first séance to allegedly contact the spirit of Houdini, and in 1972 I solved my first major case, the "haunting" of Toronto's historic Mackenzie House.

To improve my investigative skills, I spent the next two years as a private detective for a world-famous investigative agency. In addition to surveillance, bodyguarding, and other detective work, I also often went undercover to investigate cases, including arson and grand theft. Several times I was on the inside of criminal operations, including becoming a member of a warehouse theft ring. I was twice promoted.

After several other personas (blackjack dealer, newspaper stringer, riverboat manager, armed guard, Hollywood stunt trainee), I returned to the University of Kentucky for a master's degree (1982) and doctorate (1987) in English literature, with an emphasis on literary investigation and folklore. I taught part time in order to pay the bills and continued to teach until mid-1995, when I became senior research fellow of the Committee for the Scientific Investigation of Claims of the Paranormal (CSICOP), now the Committee for Skeptical Inquiry (CSI).

I have traveled the world to investigate some of its strangest mysteries. The variety of enigmas is paralleled by the different approaches needed to solve them. I have often worked with others, notably with John F. Fischer and Robert A. Baker, striving to learn more about their respective fields of forensics and psychology and coauthoring books with each. In the pages that follow we will look at the methodology of investigation, investigative strategies, rules of evidence, ethical considerations, and more as we consider a number of case studies—real examples from my X-files.

"Paranormal Investigator"— Really?

The term "paranormal investigator" has become so fashionable that sometimes it seems the PIs are everywhere. But as the following list will demonstrate, not all who style themselves as paranormal investigators are actually solving mysteries. In many instances they are doing anything but; in others, while they are engaged in honorable pursuits, they simply are not doing investigative work. Let's begin with the least credible pretender and work our way up.

1. *Mystery Monger.* This type might go on site to view some allegedly paranormal occurrence but only with the intent of fostering a mystery. The typical approach is to claim that we don't know the explanation for some alleged occurrence (a light in the sky, say), so therefore we *do* know (it's a flying saucer from another planet). This is an example of a logical fallacy called arguing from ignorance (i.e., drawing a conclusion from a lack of knowledge).

2. *Pseudoscientist.* The paranormal is rife with pseudoscience—that which superficially looks like science but fundamentally is not. Take, for example, the ubiquitous "ghost hunters" who use glitch-prone equipment for the supposed detection of spirits. In fact, the instruments do no such thing (for instance, an electromagnetic-field meter may only be responding to an old house's faulty wiring). Therefore such activity is not an "investigation" but a fool's errand.

3. *"Researcher."* This title follows the names of many who appear on TV documentaries (or "crocumentaries" as I sometimes call them). It may mean nothing more than that the person spends time at the local library in an undisciplined pursuit of fanciful ideas. Some "researchers" upgrade their title to "investigator," but they are often just cranks or mystery mongers. (Real researchers are discussed

under number 13, Research Specialist.)

4. *Rewrite Man.* In old newspaper parlance, a "rewrite man" was one who took wire-service reports from the teletype, or news turned in by reporters, and rewrote it into articles. Today, there are self-styled "paranormal investigators"—on whatever side of whatever issue—who seldom leave their computer terminals or who (as my mentor James Randi disparages) "sit back thumbing through the writings of others to glean enough information" for an article or book.

5. *Plagiarist.* The "Rewrite Man" or woman who uses another's work should give credit where it is due. It may not be necessary to cite facts that are common knowledge or are found in standard reference works, but if one is in doubt sources should be cited. Consider the case of "psychic" Sylvia Browne who has been cranking out books as "The #1 *New York Times* best-selling author." In my review of her 2005 *Secrets and Mysteries of the World* (*Skeptical Inquirer*, September/October 2005), I relate how I found one passage that bore such a striking resemblance to one of mine (concerning the Shroud of Turin) that, given the book's lack of any reference to my article, clearly shows plagiarism.

6. *Reviewer.* Writing book and movie reviews is a respectable profession (although some who have reviewed *my* books should be tarred and feathered). The same approach, however, is sometimes applied to paranormal topics so that the result is essentially a critique of some claim. This can be important educational work, but it is not paranormal investigation (unless it rises to the level of what I call an "investigative review"—one in which the critique is transformed into an investigative article).

7. *Armchair Explainer.* Some skeptical educators take a top-down approach to paranormal claims and mysteries. Although they may never have conducted an on-site investigation or talked with someone who has had a supposedly paranormal experience, they apply critical-thinking skills to explain—or explain away—the issue. The explainer often takes a "shotgun approach" to the topic, suggesting that the answer could be any of several possible explanations. (For instance, a "lake monster" might be a school of fish, a bobbing log, a wave effect, etc.) This may be useful—indeed it is sometimes the best we can do—but rounding up the usual suspects is not the same as actually solving a specific mystery. (Investigation might specifically suggest that the sighting was otters swimming in a line.)

8. *Reporter.* Sometimes one goes beyond the approach of the

Reviewer or Armchair Explainer, actually visiting a paranormal site or interviewing a claimant, witness, or expert. This may resemble detective work, but unless one honestly attempts to get to the bottom of some issue it is hardly an investigation. Some reporters are at such pains to show "both sides"—sometimes even emphasizing a pro-paranormal view in a mystery-mongering way—that the result is a non-investigation or worse.

9. *Debunker.* The end result of an honest investigation may well be to debunk—that is, to expose *bunk* or nonsense. In that sense, therefore, debunking is praiseworthy. However, to *set out* to debunk suggests one is motivated by bias against the claim rather than by a desire to honestly and fairly investigate it. (James Randi's Million Dollar Challenge to psychics and others claiming paranormal powers is not debunking, as some opponents suggest, but an invitation for claimants to submit to an investigation with the opportunity for reward if they can prove their abilities.)

10. *Prejudger.* Some believers and debunkers are sure they already know the answer to a question, pro or con, so their "investigation" consists of gathering evidence to support their prior belief. They proceed by working backward to the evidence, picking and choosing. An example of this approach is the effort of Shroud of Turin supporters to explain away the cloth's lack of historical record, the fourteenth-century forger's reported confession, the presence of pigments and paint, and the radiocarbon tests that date the cloth to the forger's time. Debunkers may be similarly prejudicial on the other side, convinced that Jesus's reputed burial cloth could not exist. However, in contrast, real science begins with the best evidence and lets it lead, with due impartiality, to the probable explanation.

11. *Stunt Performer.* A stunt is something done to gain attention. For instance, skeptics sometimes perpetrate a hoax to show how easily people are fooled—say, deceiving a newspaper editor into publishing a fake UFO photo. The risk is that when the deception is revealed, readers may not take away the intended message, instead concluding that skeptics are mean-spirited, know-it-all biased debunkers. As to the editor, he or she may never trust the skeptic again. Some stunts—such as publicly confronting superstitious taboos (e.g., breaking a mirror to challenge the proverbial seven years' bad luck)—may be educational if done properly; the approach isn't seriously investigatory. On the other hand, tricking a

dubious claimant to test his or her purported paranormal skills would be an investigative strategy.

12. *Expert.* Scholars and scientists, among other experts, sometimes examine paranormal claims; in so doing they may be most effective investigators. They may also provide expert testimony that assists an investigator in solving a case. However, outside their specialized fields, experts are only laymen and laywomen, and, as magicians well know, even the most intelligent of them can be fooled.

13. *Research Specialist.* This scientific or scholarly inquirer—in contrast to the dubious "Researcher" characterized above—is a seeker of accurate information. He or she differs from the investigator only in scope: i.e., research is the systematic seeking of knowledge, whereas investigation is targeted research gathered in the attempt to solve a mystery. (That is to say, while we "research" nineteenth-century spiritualism, we "investigate" a particular medium's suspicious "materializations.")

14. *Investigator.* Just as homicide detectives are invariably not scientists—although they may use many experts from diverse fields in solving a case—the paranormal investigator is apt rather to be someone who simply exhibits great curiosity and a talent for solving mysteries. Obviously it is helpful to have some knowledge and experience in the various fields that may apply: history of the paranormal, stage magic and mentalism, forensic science, psychology, investigative tactics and techniques, folklore, and many other subjects.

Investigation is, unfortunately, time consuming. While it could take a Mystery Monger only moments to foster a mystery, an investigator might have to spend weeks, months, or years on a case—not because the claim is good but rather because the evidence is poor, perhaps having been lost or otherwise problematic. Still, investigation is the gold standard. While we cannot investigate every haunted house or flying saucer claim and cannot examine every psychic, we can certainly investigate many cases, including the best ones, and—hopefully—solve them. Thus we may reach a provisional opinion as to the likelihood of a given phenomenon being genuine.

Methodology and Evidence

As we see, paranormal investigation consists neither of dismissiveness nor mere belief but is instead the method used to solve—to explain—mysteries of the paranormal. The results may impact cultural, historical, scientific, and other issues, or they may shed light on additional "paranormal" problems. Although some of the results may ultimately prove little more than as footnotes, they eliminate the need for further investigation, may open up new areas for research, and may enhance the interpretation of that which was already known.

Procedurally, just as with a legal problem, the investigation of a paranormal mystery may involve several potentially applicable hypotheses. As observed by David Binder and Paul Bergman in their legal text, *Fact Investigation: From Hypothesis to Proof* (1984, 162),

> Investigation is often all too readily thought of as a time to learn evidence. But remember that the evidence-gathering phase of investigation is normally preceded by analysis which ultimately dictates what evidence one pursues. This analysis concerns in part the potential legal theories and factual hypotheses that one may pursue during investigation.

Additionally, W.I.B. Beveridge—in his *The Art of Scientific Investigation* (n.d., 63)—explains the significance of hypothesis in investigation:

> Hypothesis is the most important mental technique of the investigator, and its main function is to suggest new experiments or new observations. Indeed, most experiments and many observations are carried out with the deliberate object of testing an hypothesis. Another function is to help one see the significance of an object or event that otherwise would mean nothing. For instance, a mind prepared by the hypothesis of evolution would make many more significant observations on a field

excursion than one not so prepared. Hypotheses should be used as tools to uncover new facts rather than as ends in themselves.

Essentially, the goal of the investigator—who will abandon or modify hypotheses as necessary—is to develop proof in favor of one hypothesis that is sufficient to solve the original problem. While the standard of proof or persuasion that is required to settle paranormal issues has never been codified, proof can nevertheless be characterized by analogy to the two standards used in civil law.

The first, or lower, standard—equivalent to what is styled in civil cases as "a preponderance of the evidence"—would be represented in paranormal matters by establishing *the preferred hypothesis*, among those that can be put forward, which appears sufficient to account for the evidence or at least is capable of explaining more data than are competing hypotheses.

Should there be more than a single hypothesis capable of accounting for the known facts, the investigator can determine the preferred hypothesis by invoking "Occam's razor"—named for the philosopher William of Ockham (ca. 1300–1349). Also known as the "maxim of parsimony," it affirms that the simplest viable explanation—that is the one that makes the fewest assumptions—is most likely to be correct and therefore is to be preferred (Beveridge n.d., 115–116; Shneour 1986, 310–313).

As to the second, or higher, standard of persuasion, it would be comparable to the civil law standard termed "clear and convincing evidence. (The highest legal standard, "proof beyond a reasonable doubt," is reserved for criminal cases and would seem impractical for paranormal questions—although such a standard might well be achieved [Hill et al. 1978, 49].) Such a higher standard of persuasion would naturally involve evidence of a weight significantly greater than that sufficient to establish a preferred hypothesis. Generally speaking, the "clear and convincing" standard would apply to a hypothesis that had been rigorously tested—either scientifically or critically—or that could otherwise be upgraded to the status of accepted "theory." Yet, as Martin Gardner cautions (1957, 7) "there are no known methods for giving precise 'probability values' to hypotheses."

Now, either the "preferred hypothesis" or the accepted theory may still have flaws or leave some questions unanswered. Therefore, merely raising objections is insufficient to remove it from its position of advantage. Instead, removal of a hypothesis or theory from its preferred position should come from development of a demonstrably superior hypothesis, whereupon it in turn becomes the preferred hypothesis. Of course, evidence clearly fatal to a hypothesis or theory would cause its removal even if no replacement were available.

Wherever there is controversy, it is important to consider who has the burden of proof. In law, scholarship, and science, it necessarily falls on whomever advances a claim—never on someone else to prove otherwise. (As a practical matter in legal controversies, however, Binder and Bergman [1984, 13] point out, "In most cases, despite the fact that the plaintiff has the burden of proof, both plaintiffs and defendants present affirmative as well as rebuttal evidence.") In addition, the maxim that "extraordinary claims require extraordinary proof" must apply, meaning that evidence must be proportional to the extent of a claim.

A word must be said about bias. Beveridge urges "the intellectual discipline of subordinating ideas to facts." As he explains (n.d., 67–68): "A danger constantly to be guarded against is that as soon as one formulates an hypothesis, parental affection tends to influence observations, interpretation and judgment; 'wishful thinking' is likely to start unconsciously." He adds, "The best protection against these tendencies is to cultivate an intellectual habit of subordinating one's opinions and wishes to objective evidence and a reverence for things as they really are, and to keep constantly in mind that the hypothesis is only a supposition."

Here is a concise summary of the steps by which skeptics—as opposed to True Believers or their polar opposites, debunkers—advance science and reason through inquiry, investigation, and use of the scientific method. It is outlined by the acronym SKEPTICISM:

> Science
> Knowledge
> Evidence
> Postulations
> Testing
> Impartiality
> Criticism
> Investigation
> Solving
> Mastery

That is, with *science* as a basis, one approaches some question or mystery using past *knowledge* and acquired *evidence* to form *postulations* (or hypotheses) which undergo *testing* to rank them, with *impar-*

tiality (i.e., guarding against bias) and *criticism* (the act of making judgments), finally conducting an *investigation* (targeted research) that results in *solving* (or determining the most likely explanation for) the mystery at hand, providing *mastery* over it.

Thus we gain mastery over mystery. Indeed, as I like to say, we can see the progress of science as a series of solved mysteries.

Notes on Argument and Logic

An investigator must present his or her arguments persuasively. Therefore it is necessary to use the tools of argument, including induction and deduction, and to avoid logical fallacies.

Inductive reasoning begins with particular facts and moves to general conclusions. The process involves observing a group of facts and developing a hypothesis to explain them, then investigating to confirm or disprove the hypothesis.

Deductive reasoning is a movement in the opposite direction: One begins with a general principle (often arrived at by induction), applies it to a fact, and so draws a conclusion about that fact. Deductive reasoning is best illustrated with a syllogism:

1. All cats are mammals.
2. Fifi is a cat.
3. Therefore, Fifi is a mammal

However, if you switch the second and third statements, you create an invalid syllogism:

1. All cats are mammals.
2. Fifi is a mammal.
3. Therefore, Fifi is a cat.

In fact, Fifi might be a poodle or other mammal.

Both induction and deduction contain potential pitfalls, called *logical fallacies*. These include the following:

1. *Post hoc, ergo propter hoc* ("after this, therefore, because of this"). It is a fallacy to assume that, simply because an event follows another event, the first was the cause of the second. More evidence

than time sequence is needed for establishing a causal relationship.

2. *Argumentum ad ignorantiam* ("an argument from ignorance"). Para-normal claims are very, very frequently based on this fallacy, which involves drawing a conclusion from a lack of knowledge: for example, "We don't know what the noise in the old house was; therefore, it must have been a ghost."

3. *Argumentum ad hominem* ("an argument to the man"). This fallacy consists of attacking one's opponent rather than dealing with the issue under discussion.

Other logical fallacies include an argument from authority (asserting that something is true because a supposed authority says so), false di-chotomy (suggesting there are just two possibilities when there may be others), and more: See "Top 20 Logical Fallacies" on *The Skeptics Guide to the Universe* (online at http://www.theskepticsguide.org/resources/logical fallacies.aspx).

Some Ethical Concerns

The investigative approach is nothing less than a quest for the truth. That is why the Committee for Skeptical Inquiry has, from its inception, refused to reject claims antecedent to inquiry but instead calls for them to be examined carefully and with due objectivity and impartiality. In short, mysteries should neither be fostered nor dismissed but investigated with a view toward solving them.

In conducting investigations over more than four decades, I have sought to act ethically, and I have come to advocate an approach that is humanistic as well as scientific—that is, one that is respectful of people who deserve respect. All too often a skeptic, especially one of the "debunker" stripe, will tap his or her head to indicate that a claimed alien abductee is deranged or make a gesture simulating drinking to suggest a UFO eyewitness may have been intoxicated. But many paranormal experiencers are sane and sober, as well as intelligent and sincere. They deserve, when possible, to have their experience investigated and explained—not to find themselves tarred with a false accusation.

Of course, those who mislead others must be challenged, but investigators are urged to avoid—or at least employ extreme caution in using—the f-word, *fraud*. Doing so shifts the burden of proof to the accuser, who must not only disprove the claim but prove the claimant intended to deceive. If the claimant is only mistaken, the accuser is therefore guilty of defamation.

Because investigators are seeking truth, it is generally counterproductive for them to perpetrate a hoax—say launching a fake flying saucer in the form of a balloon with blinking lights. Such hoaxes tend to appeal most to debunkers; others are not so likely to get the desired message—i.e., that people are easily fooled—but are instead apt to conclude that the tricksters are just mean-spirited jerks.

Similarly objectionable, I believe, is for the investigator to pose as a medium, pretending to talk with people's dead loved ones, and then revealing the deception in order to show how easily they can be deceived. I avoid this approach for a variety of reasons, largely because of ethical concerns. I agree with Houdini (1924, xi), who did spiritualistic stunts early in his career:

> At the time I did such stunts, I appreciated the fact that I had surprised my clients, but though aware of the fact I was *deceiving* them, I did not see or understand the seriousness of trifling with such sacred sentimentality—or the unfortunate results that inevitably followed. To me it was a lark. I was a mystifier, my ambition was being gratified, and my love of a mild sensation was being satisfied. After delving deep, though, I realized the seriousness of it all. As I advanced to riper years of experience, I came to realize the seriousness of trifling with the hallowed reverence the average human being bestows on the departed. When I personally became afflicted with similar grief, I was chagrined that I had ever been guilty of such frivolity; for the first time, I realized that it borders on crime.

Of course, tricking people in order to educate them is not the same as deceiving them for crass personal gain. As a "mentalist" I have convinced children I could read minds, then confessed otherwise to teach them about deception, and I once taught a Hollywood actress to do fortunetelling tricks as part of a TV documentary for a similar purpose.

However, when one ethically motivated writer ventured to criticize *any* deception by a skeptic—including using a false persona to test an alleged psychic—I was asked to respond. (See *Skeptical Inquirer* January/February 2007, 67–68). I pointed out that when I worked undercover as a private detective, I saw proof of the old maxim that one must "set a thief to catch a thief." Since many paranormal claimants refuse to be tested under meaningful conditions, I believe surreptitious tests are permissable. If the claimants are genuine, they have nothing to fear from such tests.

Investigative Strategies

Apart from general guidelines about formulating hypotheses and avoiding bias, it is difficult to say just how an investigation should be conducted. Still, there are some generalized strategies that have proved effective. They will at least provide some options to consider and will surely stimulate the thought process.

1. *Investigate on site.* My first serious case, the "haunting" at historic Mackenzie House in Toronto in 1972, instilled in me the importance of this approach. Among the reported phenomena there were footsteps on the stairs and the sounds of William Lyon Mackenzie's antique printing press rumbling and clattering in the cellar. A printing press; would it seem relevant that next door was a publishing company?

Actually, such jumping to a conclusion from an armchair does not solve the mystery, since the adjacent building had no presses (it only held offices and warehouse space). As I learned, however, by visiting the scene, the noises did come from that building. The "printing press" sounds were caused by the late-night cleanup crew dragging heavy iron-wheeled carts, loaded with rattling metal garbage cans, across the rough concrete floor. As to the footsteps on the Mackenzie House stairs, they actually occurred on the adjacent metal staircase (the two sets of stairs were only some forty inches apart), produced by the same workmen or, alternately, by the building's caretaker or his family. (See my *Secrets of the Supernatural*, 1988, 17–27.)

For another case of investigating on site, see my examination of the "statues with heartbeats" (Nickell 2007a, 225–226).

2. *Check details of an account.* There is an old skeptics' saying—a "skepticalism"—that goes like this: Before you try to explain something, make sure it really happened. Take the case of the notorious

"Amityville Horror" house, for instance. After Ronald DeFeo murdered his parents and siblings there in 1974, it was purchased the following year by George Lutz and his wife Kathy. Soon, there was a popular book by Jan Anson, *The Amityville Horror: A True Story* (1977), describing how demonic forces had damaged doors and windows and even left cloven hoofprints in the snow, among many other claims.

In fact, the "true story" was no such thing. I interviewed Barbara Cromarty who purchased the house with her husband James after it was given up by the Lutzes. It turned out that there had been no such damage and that all the old hardware was still in place. Other researchers discovered that the footprints claim was also bogus, since weather reports revealed there had been no snowfall at the time claimed. Eventually, DeFeo's attorney, William Weber, admitted that he and the Lutzes had "created this horror story over many bottles of wine that George Lutz was drinking" (see Nickell 2004, 73–77).

Another case in which it was crucial to check the alleged facts was that of the incredible disappearance of Oliver Lerch (related in my *Secrets of the Supernatural* (Nickell with Fischer 1988, 61–73) and in my *The Magic Detectives* (Nickell 1989, 84–86).

3. *Research precedents.* It can be helpful to look at similar cases— those with features like those of the case at hand—that have already been solved. Consider, for instance, the Mystery of the Newberry Demon. Given in the writings of Puritan minister Increase Mather (1639–1723), the incidents began at a home in Newbury, Massachusetts, in 1679. There, physical disturbances—which Mather thought were the works of a demon or possibly the Devil himself—seemed to center around a young boy. He suffered violent fits, shaking or jumping up and down, and at times he would bark like a dog or cluck like a hen. Ashes were put into the family's food, an iron hammer was thrown at the grandfather, and objects, such as a chest, were moved from their resting places. Then, a visiting seaman said that if he could have the boy for a day, he would put an end to the troubles. The grandfather agreed, and the sailor kept his promise. Did he perform some type of exorcism, or did he do something quite simple?

A study of many such "poltergeist" cases reveals that such destructive phenomena are typically centered, as in the Newbury case, around an unhappy child, adolescent, or immature adult. In many cases the juvenile is caught surreptitiously throwing an object or causing other mischief. Whenever the problem is recognized and his or her unhappiness alleviated, the phenomena usually cease. At Newbury, the fact that the disturbances did not continue when the boy was away from home and that it ceased completely after the sailor had a talk with him provides convincing evidence that he was responsible. No doubt the wise seaman made it clear that—unlike the superstitious Puritan adults—he was not fooled by the childish pranks. He probably convinced the lad that it was wrong to cause such mischief and lent a sympathetic ear to the boy's troubles. The fact that the child was living with his grandparents, rather than his parents, could indicate that his family life had been disrupted, and he was unhappy about it (see Nickell 1995, 97–103).

4. *Carefully examine physical evidence.* The message here is the importance of collecting available evidence and examining it carefully (commissioning an expert examination when appropriate). Consider the case of a "spirit painting"—a large (40" by 60") oil portrait of an alleged spirit guide named Azur (Figure 1)—that spirits purportedly pro-

Figure 1. "Spirit" oil painting of Azur, produced in stages during an 1898 séance (exhibited at the Maplewood Hotel, Lily Dale).

Figure 2. Surface damage is apparent in each of the four corners of the Azur painting—a possible indication of trickery. (Photos by Joe Nickell)

duced in stages during an 1898 séance. (The medium and canvas were in an area of the séance room that was screened from the sitters by a curtain. They were brought in one at a time to view the alleged spirit work in progress.) But how could such an elaborate painting have been done by trickery in low-light conditions and in just an hour and a half?

I was able to examine the painting at Lily Dale, the spiritualist community in western New York, and rule out some techniques of fakery. However, I did discover in each of the four corners evidence of surface damage (Figure 2)—consistent with one fake spirit-painting technique. In this the phoney medium has previously prepared the painting and, when dry, has covered it with a piece of blank canvas (such as by adhering it to each corner), which is then removed during the séance. Since the painting was allegedly done in increments, the medium could have produced some stages on the blank canvas during the séance, or there may even have been two or more overlays to represent different stages. (See Nickell 2001, 259–266.)

5. *Analyze development of a phenomenon.* This strategy aims to show the big picture—sometimes literally. Beginning in the 1970s, great circular designs began to appear mysteriously in the grain fields of southern England. Theories to explain them ranged from flying-saucer touchdowns to wind vortexes. However, the examination of this or that "crop circle"—in which the plant stems were laid down in a swirled pattern—revealed little, other than negative evidence: the reported absence of footprints or damage to plants—all of which added to the enigma.

I recalled the old adage about not seeing the forest for the trees and suggested an examination—not of one or another crop circle but of the phenomenon itself. Working with forensic analyst John Fischer, I found four revealing aspects of the proliferating circles, based on data spanning several years: (1) The circles were growing in number each year, roughly correlating with increasing media reports; (2) they were increasing in complexity (from simple swirled circles to circles with rings and satellites to ever more complex geometric patterns, "pictographs," and so on); they were geographically limited to southern England (except when media reports spread their occurrence to other countries, including the United States, Canada, and Japan); and they exhibited a "shyness effect" (meaning they appeared at night in fields away from farmhouses). The evidence was most consistent with the hypothesis of hoaxing, and, as we prepared to publish our findings, "two jovial con men in their sixties" came forward to admit they had made many of the early circles and had been copied by others. (The lack of footprints and crop damage was attributable to hoaxers walking the tracks left by sprayers, and to the pliability of green plant stalks. (See Nickell 2001, 70–82.)

For another example of analyzing the development of a phenomenon, see my iconographic study of the evolution of the extraterrestrial likeness in popular culture (Nickell 2001, 160–164).

6. *Assess a claim with a controlled test or experiment.* In 1976, while living in Dawson City, Yukon (site of the famous Klondike gold rush)—where I worked as a casino dealer and riverboat manager—I got to

know four local dowsers, including an employer, Captain Dick Stevenson. All claimed to be able to use their witching wands and pendulums to locate gold, although one wondered aloud that, if so, why weren't they rich?

I assembled the group on one of the famous old gold claims. My test was simple: Into several small, identical cardboard boxes I placed a gold nugget or another test item—or nothing at all. To rule out any subterranean influence, I had the dowsers ply their rods over the area and satisfy themselves there was none. Each then tried his supposed ability on a group of boxes (which I scrambled by mixing them in a large bag, then drew them out one at a time and placed them in a row, several inches apart, on some end-to-end planks). I recorded the guesses of each turn, then repeated the test with a second series of boxes. The results were abysmal: they could not tell gold from fool's gold or anything else, being wrong seven times for every time they were correct. (See Nickell with Fischer 1988, 89–102.)

7. *Consider an innovative analysis.* Sometimes a unique problem invites a creative solution. A case in point is the repeated eyewitness descriptions of "lake monsters" as exceedingly long, serpentine creatures swimming in an undulating manner.

However, some eyewitnesses have later recognized that what they actually saw were otters swimming in a line. In addition to collecting their testimony and studying the phenomenon, I decided to see how well monster-inhabited lakes and rivers correlated with otter populations. I prepared a map of North America onto which I superimposed both sets of data with the result that a very strong correlation could be seen. This was not meant to suggest that all lake-monster sightings are of otters, but it does show that the creatures are excellent candidates for certain sightings. (See Nickell 2007c.)

8. *Attempt to recreate the "impossible."* Frequently some paranormal claim is made on the basis that human beings could not have produced some effect or, if they did, they must have had paranormal assistance. Take, for instance, the enigmatic lines and giant figures of animals that are drawn on the Nasca plain in Peru that have been attributed to "ancient astronauts." Indeed, the drawings or "geoglyphs" are so large they can only be properly viewed from the air, so if they were made by ancient Nasca people, how did they engineer such large effigies?

To answer that question, I attempted to recreate one of the largest figures, the giant "condor" measuring 440 feet long. Without sophisticated equipment (using only sticks and knotted cord) and without advanced techniques (e.g., the measurement of angles), six of us were able to replicate the figure—by enlargement from a six-foot drawing— in just two days. According to *Scientific American* ("Big Picture" 1983), it was "remarkable in its exactness" to the Nasca original. (See Nickell 2007a, 151–158.) I later recreated the giant Nasca spider for National Geographic Television's *Is It Real?* (See Nickell 2007d.)

For other examples of recreating the "impossible," see my work on the Shroud of Turin (Nickell 1998), and the "miraculous blood" of St. Januarius (Nickell 1992, 145–164).

9. *Go undercover to investigate.* The book *Psychic Mafia* by M. Lamar Keene (1976) exposed the tricks of phoney mediums, largely at the notorious Camp Chesterfield in Indiana. Over the years came other exposées there, but in the summer of 2001 I wondered if the spiritualists at Camp Chesterfield were still up to their old tricks. They were. I went undercover there and at other sites with the intention of testing the claims of "psychic mediums" and the like, and of uncovering and possible deceptive practices. Undercover work is discussed at some length in the following chapter.

Undercover

Scientists, magicians, and other skeptics have frequently gone under-cover to expose paranormal charlatans—spiritualists especially.

One determined investigator in the 1850s went undercover at an on-stage séance conducted by the notorious Davenport Brothers. The duo, Ira and William, had themselves tied up in a "spirit cabinet" by volunteers from the audience. After the doors were shut and the lights turned down, spectators witnessed phantom hands waving from the cabinet and heard the sounds of musical instruments that had been placed inside. Afterward, the men were still securely tied. One of the volunteers, a printer by trade, had come prepared with some printer's ink, and after the Davenports were tied he smeared some of the black paste on the neck of a violin. When the séance ended, one of the pair was discovered to have his shoulder besmeared with the tell-tale sub-stance (Nickell 2001, 25).

Harry Houdini (1874–1926), the great magician and escape artist who crusaded against spiritualists' deceptions, sometimes went un-dercover, using his magical skills to detect—and even boobytrap—their fraudulent productions. To avoid being recognized, Houdini (1924) utilized disguise—donning a wig, heavy glasses, shabby clothes, and whatever else fit his false persona. He also sent out showgirls and other undercover agents whom he later termed "my own secret serv-ice" (Kalush and Sloman 2006, 454–455). One, as "Florence B. Rush"—Rose Mackenberg—sat in hundreds of séances and even became an ordained spiritualist minister six times. She posed masterfully as a jeal-ous wife, neurotic schoolmarm, factory worker, widow, or other per-sona—arriving in a city ten days before Houdini to obtain inside information for his exposées (Kalush and Sloman 2006, 460–461).

Other investigators have followed suit. In 1956 magician Milbourne Christopher used a false name, "John Banks," to assess a supposedly telepathic horse named Lady Wonder. The mare had impressed ESP pioneer Dr. J.B. Rhine with her apparent ability. Alas, when Christopher inquired of Lady, "What is my name?" the mare obligingly nudged the appropriate letters of a large typewriter-like contraption to spell B-A-N-K-S, and Christopher (1970, 39–54) saw that the horse's trainer, Mrs. Claudia Fonda, was secretly cueing her charge. (Lady was trained to sway her head over the letters and, when she was over the correct one, Mrs. Fonda gave a "slight movement" of her training rod, signaling the animal to nudge that letter.)

James Randi and various colleagues used false personas and disguises to uncover faith-healing scams in the lead-up to Randi's book *The Faith Healers* (1987). One of the investigators, Paul Kurtz (1994, 321–325), relates a hilarious anecdote about his own false mustache, which he wore when he investigated the Rev. W.V. Grant in Rochester. Loosened by the mayonnaise from a sandwich, the mustache drooped, and finally he removed it. Soon, a credulous audience member seated next to him, misunderstanding the reason for the change in his appearance, remarked that the "healing" service was already making him look younger! Another investigator, Don Henvick—who transformed himself into a remarkably homely "Bernice Manicoff"—was "healed" of uterine cancer at a Peter Popoff service (Steiner 1986, 31).

Randi himself, suspicious about Popoff's need for a hearing aid, smuggled into one the evangelist's services an electronics expert with computerized scanning equipment. They discovered that Popoff's remarkable ability to divine what ailed audience members—supposedly by a supernatural "word of knowledge"—was simply Mrs. Popoff, backstage, reading from so-called prayer cards attendees filled out before the service. She broadcast the information to Rev. Popoff's "hearing aid" (Steiner 1986, 1989; Randi 1987, 141–149).

My own undercover work began in the 1970s when I was an operative for a world-famous detective agency. My garb was simply that of whatever role I was playing: work clothes for forklift driver and shipper-receiver; ditto with hard hat, leather gloves, safety goggles, and steel-toed shoes as steelworker; salmon-colored lab coat for lens polisher; rolled-up shirt sleeves and a change apron as a tavern waiter; and so on. My only use of disguise was on non-undercover assignments, doing such extensive surveillance of a subject that I occasionally needed to make minor alterations to my appearance (such as adding eyeglasses and using a reversible jacket) to minimize my recognizability.

When I became a full-time paranormal investigator for CSI in 1995, I began to appear frequently on television and was soon being recognized on occasion when visiting certain sites. Sometimes that could be helpful, but in other cases it could prove detrimental, for example inhibiting the proper testing of an alleged psychic or the uncovering of séance trickery.

So it was in 2001 that I decided to use a disguise and false name when I visited the notorious spiritualist enclave, Camp Chesterfield in Indiana. The place had been the target of many exposés, notably the book *The Psychic Mafia* by a confessed fraudulent medium (Keene 1976). Skeptical reporters visiting the grounds have been assaulted and evicted bodily (Keene 1976, 48–49). And I had recently been on national TV, helping *Dateline NBC* expose "psychic medium" John Edward and so presumably attracting the ire of Chesterfield's mediums. So I shaved my mustache and otherwise altered my appearance, and as "Jim Collins" I limped onto the grounds with a cane for a week's stay. I uncovered bogus readings, alleged spirit productions, and other deceptions (Nickell 2004, 31–45). At one session involving "billet readings," sitters wrote on slips of paper the names of deceased loved ones along with a question ("Mother will you be with me always?" I wrote). Because it was requested that all slips be folded in the same way, the medium could hold one slip to his forehead while (hidden by the lectern) surreptitiously unfolding and reading from another. For me he read off the names I'd given and passed on a loving answer to my question, supposedly from my mother. It was very moving until I remembered that at that time my mother was still living and wasn't named Mrs. Collins! I was further consoled by having caught another phoney who preyed on the bereaved. (See my "Undercover Among the Spirits" presented later in this book as a case study.)

Again, in 2003 I adopted the false persona of a homely old yokel with suitable garb, altered appearance, and the name "Johnny Adams" in order to check out well-known paranormal claimant, Phil Jordan, who works as an alleged psychic medium and sometimes crime-solving clairvoyant. But Jordan not only made meaningless pronouncements in the reading he did for me, he failed to mention such life-transforming events as my mother's Alzheimer's or the discovery of a daughter and grandchildren I had not known about. He not only failed to see through my false persona, but he even autographed a copy of his book to his friend "Johnny." I called Jordan the "psychic sleuth without a clue" (Nickell 2007, 231–235).

Yet again, working with National Geographic Television's *Is It Real?* series, I went on an investigation of a Brazilian faith healer known as John of God at an April 4, 2006, appearance in Atlanta. He claims to be possessed by spirit entities who help direct treatments for the afflicted. Doing a makeover that included wearing the event's requisite all-white garb, I adopted the persona of a pilgrim seeking a miracle cure. John of God singled me out for a special "invisible" procedure, but he failed to recognize that my affliction was a sham and that I was working on an exposé of his bogus claims. (See my "John of God: Healings by Entities?," *Skeptical Inquirer*, September/October 2007, 20–22).

Other undercover faith-healing investigations included attending healing services of such evangelists as Benny Hinn (Nickell 2004, 261–269), and the notorious Peter Popoff, who was back on the circuit after Randi's effective exposé (Nickell 2007, 95–102). (On one visit to a basilica in Lackawanna, New York, to see a traveling eucharistic-miracles exhibit, I participated, in impromptu fashion and thus without disguise, in a healing service, as shown in the accompanying photo [Figure 1].)

On still other occasions, I have used disguise to avoid recognition, such as when accompanied by a *New Yorker* magazine reporter to another spiritualist camp where I happened to be well-known (Bilger 2002). Once I used my experience to help transform a Hollywood actress into the persona of a psychic for a documentary that exposed the tricks of phoney readers. I also once adopted the persona of a terminal prostate-

Figure 1. The author "going under the power"—actually having been pushed by the Catholic evangelical—at a healing service in upstate New York. (Author's photo by Diana Gawen Harris.)

cancer patient in Tijuana—first, for a visit to a fortuneteller, then for another to a hospital where I was offered options ranging from prayer to quack treatments such as the use of Laetrile (Nickell 2007, 189–191, 239–241).

In 2006, the Hollywood-based Independent Investigations Group (IIG)—for whom I once conducted an investigative workshop and who gave me their 2009 "Houdini Award"—used false personas to test prominent "psychic detective" Carla Baron. Several IIG members attended a seminar featuring Baron, who selected three of them for "personal readings," but she never "picked up on the fact," writes Brian Hart (2006), "that none of us were who we claimed to be." For example, "A computer consultant fed her the false scenario that he was a screenwriter, and she went into quite an elaborate and detailed story about what he was to expect from his soon-to-be successful (nonexistent) screenplay."

As these examples show—and many more could be given—under-cover work is a useful investigative technique. Although anything can be abused, if conducted properly such an approach is analogous to that used by police and private detectives to uncover certain criminal activity. Often, there is no really effective substitute.

The Investigator's Kit

Although the serious investigator will be best prepared by having a trained mind, in addition some specific equipment will often prove useful.

Perhaps the first paranormal investigator's kit was that used by England's Harry Price (1936), the father of modern "ghost hunting." Among his gadgetry was "a sensitive transmitting thermograph, with charts, to measure the slightest variation in temperature in supposed haunted rooms."

Figure 1. Some essential investigative tools are kept by the author in his trousers and sport-coat pockets, including, on the left, a notebook, pen, and evidence-collection kit, and on the right, a combination knife, digital camera, and penlighted loupe.

Figure 2. Field kit, utilizing a "catalog" case together with camera, stereomicroscope, and various modules: smaller, special-purpose kits that may be included in the larger kit as needed.

Following Price's lead, today's pseudoscientific, would-be investigators often take technological gadgets to sites of alleged "paranormal activity" in search of otherworldly "energy." Various "ghost hunters," for example, use everything from geiger counters to dowsing rods to electromagnetic-field (EMF) meters, without seeming to realize that such devices are not only not made to detect ghosts but do not in fact do so. EMF meters, for instance, may simply be responding to faulty wiring or a nearby microwave tower (Nickell 2006, 25–26).

More sensibly, the scientific investigator will find several items useful for fieldwork—notably materials for notetaking and photographing. Additional equipment will occasionally prove useful: a tape recorder (not to detect ghostly "EVPs" [electronic voice phenomena] but to record interviews), a camcorder (for visually recording some activity, such as a dowser's efforts), and even more specialized equipment (Baker and Nickell 1992, 83–88). A tape measure and a lensatic compass will be useful for some fieldwork—such as examining a crop circle (Nickell 2007, 11–16). I always have in my pockets a small notebook and pen, a compact digital camera, a penlight magnifier, a combination knife, and a little trace-evidence collection packet (see Figure 1). A photographer's-style vest, with its many pockets, will make it easy to carry many items.

I also often use a field kit constituted as needed. I have developed a *modular approach* to the kit, by which I have a number of smaller kits

Figure 3. A disguise kit may prove useful for undercover investigations. (Photos by Joe Nickell.)

(Figure 2) that are pre-assembled for various specific investigative purposes (for example, one contains the materials for making a plaster cast of a "monster" footprint). This kit-within-a-kit approach makes it possible for me to assemble what I may need for an investigation at a moment's notice.

In the past, my "weeping-icon kit," for example, has contained photographic equipment and a stereomicroscope (removed from its base, then packed in bubble wrap), in addition to an evidence-collection module that has bulb pipettes, bibulous laboratory paper, flint-glass vials, etc., plus a baloney sandwich. I used this for instance to collect samples from a tearful Toronto icon at the request of the Greek Orthodox Church and transfer them to the Ontario Provincial Police Fraud Squad for testing (Nickell 2001, 214–218).

The serious investigator may also require a disguise kit (Figure 3).

CSI: Paranormal

The popular TV series *CSI: Crime Scene Investigation* (along with its spin-offs, *CSI: New York* and *CSI: Miami*) has led the public to appreciate how forensic science can solve crimes (even if the fictional show often gets ahead of state-of-the-art forensics).

Certainly, we have come a long way since the time of the first real-life "scientific detective," an Austrian lawyer named Hans Gross (1847–1915), who seemed to bring to life Sherlock Holmes's fictional ability to glean much from a bit of evidence others had overlooked. Gross's 1893 *Handbuch fur Untersuchungsrichter* ("manual for examining magistrates," eventually published in English as *Criminal Investigation*) advocated the use of forensic medicine, serology, toxicology, ballistics, and anthropometry (the science of measuring the human body, which was used for identification until it was supplanted by fingerprinting). Gross coined the term *criminalistics* and later launched the forensic journal *Kriminologie*.

A disciple of Gross, Edmond Locard (1877–1966), set forth the concept known as Locard's Exchange Principle, which states that a cross-transfer of trace evidence occurs when the perpetrator of a crime comes into contact with a victim, an object, or a crime scene. For example, Locard proved a case against three suspected counterfeiters when he discovered tiny metal particles on their clothing and used chemical analysis to prove the particles had the same metallic elements as the bogus coins. Confronted with the scientific evidence, the arrested men confessed (Nickell and Fischer 1999, 8–10).

I have long endeavored to apply forensic techniques to the paranormal (and I can now remind readers that "CSI" is not only an acronym for Crime Scene Investigation but also for Committee for Skeptical Inquiry).

The following are synopses of some of my cases over the past four decades that illustrate how particular forensic applications helped solve strange mysteries.

Serological Tests

An early case that I took on in 1978 represented my first direct encounter with a claimed paranormal origin of blood. It involved an eastern Kentucky farmhouse with a curious address: "Deadening Branch." The deserted house had a front door that reportedly bled—indeed it had mysterious streaks that were said to correlate with a century-old tragedy: a boy crushed to death in a cane-mill mishap was reportedly "laid out" on the door before being buried in the cemetery overlooking the site. Here was a popular folklore motif, the "ineradicable bloodstain after bloody tragedy."

In fact, the greyish streaks visible on the door were consistent with water-borne substances—such as dirt, possibly tar, decaying leaves, etc.—washing down from the roof. Nevertheless, I lightly scraped off some of the deposit and carefully wrapped it in paper for future testing. This was carried out by forensic analyst John F. Fischer. He conducted several preliminary tests for various hemoglobin-related compounds, using reagents that yield color reactions in the presence of the compounds. Several such tests were negative, indicating no blood was present, even in trace amounts. When mysterious noises and other phenomena that made up the "haunting" were explained, the case gave up the ghost. (See Nickell with Fischer 1988, 119–128.)

Blood-Pattern Analysis

The mystery of Atlanta's "House of Blood" began on September 8, 1987, in the southwestern part of the city. At the home of an elderly black couple, blood began to flow from the walls and spring up from the floor "like a sprinkler." The police were called, and although they took color crime-scene photos, they abandoned the case after determining that no crime had occurred. Soon, however, accounts of the "unexplained" case began to circulate. Facts were exaggerated and the bizarre phenomenon was attributed to poltergeist activity.

I investigated the occurrence in 1991, obtaining special access to the police file and discussing the case (on and off the record) with homicide commander Lt. Horace Walker. From the photographs it did not appear to me that the blood had manifested in the manner described, so I submitted copies of the photo to a nationally recognized forensic blood-pattern analyst, Judith Bunker. Her subsequent report detailed how the blood had been applied in "spurt" patterns onto the floor and walls, giving the lie to the witnesses' statements and supporting other evidence that suggested a hoax. As one police investigator said somewhat cryptically, "Some adults will act like children just to get attention." (See "House of Blood," Nickell 1995, 92–97.)

Forensic Light Sources

In 1985, about forty persons paid twenty dollars each to attend a séance in Lexington, Kentucky, in which "spirit precipitations on silk" were produced. The "medium" placed an open bottle of ink on a table and, as the attendees sat in the darkened room, each had a small square of cloth placed in his or her lap. After a suitable invocation of spirits, who then supposedly spoke through the entranced channeler, he went about the room with a lamp that had a dim red bulb. This created an erie effect as each person turned over his or her square of cloth to reveal three or four thumbprint-sized "spirit" faces that had seemingly materialized on the fabric.

A young woman who had attended the séance came to me, feeling she had been scammed. I had her cloth swatch examined by forensic analyst John F. Fischer. Infrared and ultraviolet light showed nothing, but argon laser light revealed a tell-tale circular area around each face: this was evidence of a different type of spirit—a solvent such as ammonia or alcohol—used to transfer a newspaper or magazine photo onto fabric, with the aid of a hot iron. Obviously, blank swatches were shown the sitters but, after the lights were turned out, those were switched for prepared ones. The book *The Psychic Mafia* (Keene 1976, 64–66) tells how such fakes were made at the spiritualist Camp Chesterfield in Indiana—the very place the medium in question hailed from. I obtained police warrants against him, but the small fee he had charged each victim kept the offence within the misdemeanor range, and therefore he could not be extradited. However, he did not again ply his fraud in Kentucky. (See Nickell with Fischer 1988, 47–60.)

Microscopy

After appearing on a live episode of *Oprah* on Good Friday 1995, I sat in a limousine waiting for a ride to the Chicago airport, talking with a self-styled visionary who had also been on the program. She showed me a rose petal, supposedly from the Philippines, that bore a "miraculous" image of Jesus. After a cursory examination with my penlighted loupe, I asked to borrow the item for more careful study.

Back at my lab, I used a stereomicroscope to view the petal using transmitted light (i.e., placing it on a fluorescent light box [Figure 1]). I noted that wherever there were lines and hatch marks composing the image there was damage consistent with that made from a blunt tool. By simple experimentation I discovered that I could easily draw on rose petals with a stylus, thus producing faces with characteristics like those of the questioned one. The evidence was consistent with a pious fraud, not a miraculous occurrence. (See Nickell 2001, 105–108.)

Fingerprinting

In 1903 a young African American man named Will West was admitted to Leavenworth Penitentiary in Kansas. When technicians recorded his Bertillon measurements (length and breadth of skull, length of outstretched arms, and nine other measurements—then used in an anthropometric system of criminal identification), another man's file came up: It was that of a "William West" whose photographs looked like those of the first man. There were, however, two men. Brought together, Will and William West looked as alike as twins but were said to be unrelated. The case proved a triumph for the new science of fingerprinting, which could infallibly distinguish one man from the other.

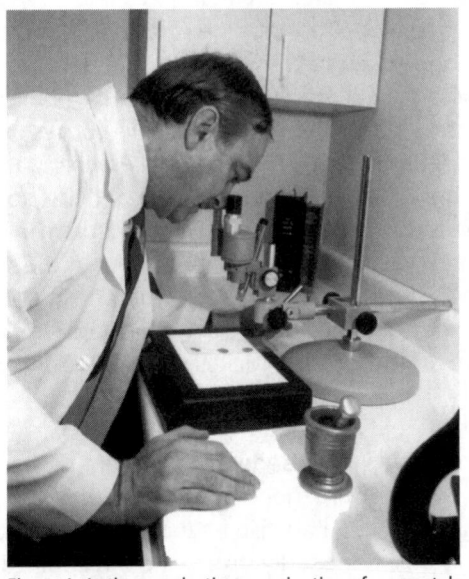

Figure 1. Author conducting examination of rose petals in CSI laboratory using stereomicroscope.

However, was the case really "one of the strangest coincidences in all history" as one source asserted?

I hypothesized that the men were identical twins. Today the matter would be settled by DNA tests, but I had to be creative to test my hypothesis. I obtained the two sets of fingerprint patterns (courtesy of the FBI) and submitted them to experts in twins' fingerprints—a field of study based on the fact that there are genetic influences on dermal ridge patterns. The Wests' pattern types proved to be so similar as to put the probability of their monozygotic (one-egg or "identical") twinship at an astronomical level. So did their likewise similar ear configurations, plus the matching Bertillon measurements. Corroborative evidence came from similar biographical details, the testimony of a fellow prisoner who knew the men to be twin brothers, and the Wests' correspondence logs, which revealed that while in Leavenworth they wrote to the same brother, the same five sisters, and the same Uncle George! My report was published in the *Journal of Police Science and Administration* (see Nickell with Fischer 1988, 75–88), and I later presented my findings to an appreciative audience at an international forensic identification conference.

DNA

A strange fetal specimen, preserved in a jar lodged in a cabinet in a natural-history museum in Saxony, has been termed "Germany's greatest mystery." It can be traced to the year 1735 when a 28-year-old woman was to give birth to her fourth child but instead produced a stillborn fetus subsequently preserved and studied by a Leipzig physician. Some fringe paranormalists attribute its abnormalities—which have earned it the local sobriquet "chicken man"—to extraterrestrial hybridization.

On a trip to Germany in 2002, I was able to visit the museum in Waldenburg with Martin Mahner, who has a doctorate in zoology. Museologist Ulrike Budig unlocked the cabinet's glass doors so we could examine and photograph the fetal specimen from various angles. We were also able to study the results of genetic tests that had been conducted by experts in Berlin and Heidelberg. They used comparative genomic hybridization, which showed that large parts of chromosome 17 were missing. This could cause the rare deformation in the embryo which, despite its inherently lethal condition, developed until the third trimester of the pregnancy. The studies clearly proved that the specimen has only human DNA, refuting the "alien-hybrid" notion. (See Nickell 2004, 46–50.)

Questioned-document Examination

The "MJ-12" documents are a group of sensational papers that supposedly prove a government cover-up regarding the 1947 "Roswell Incident"—a case of an alleged crashed flying saucer and recovered alien bodies. For example, among the papers was a memorandum to the secretary of defense bearing the authentic-appearing signature of President Harry S. Truman. The documents surfaced in 1987 on a roll of film, sent anonymously to obscure UFOlogist Jamie Shandera who in turn shared them with Roswell researchers William L. Moore and Stanton T. Friedman.

That the documents were available only on film was suspicious. It effectively precluded examination of the paper and ink, and many researchers suspected the text and markings were simply done with old typewriters in conjunction with a cut-and-paste technique, using photocopied elements from genuine documents. Several examiners contributed to the case. My involvement was encouraged by Jerome Clark of the Center for UFO Studies. Examination revealed suspicious format errors in the Truman memo, erroneous pseudomilitary date features in an alleged Eisenhower briefing paper, and other glaring errors. The Truman signature proved to have been transplanted, by photocopying from a genuine Truman letter of October 1, 1947—a fact established forensically. The credulous Friedman thought the correspondence of one signature to another was proof of authenticity; instead, it was proof of spuriousness, since no two signatures are ever *exactly* alike (see Nickell with Fischer 1992, 81–105).

Forensic Linguistics

In 1904 appeared a little pamphlet titled *A Message from Robert G. Ingersoll Transmitted by Automatic Writing Through a Philadelphia Psychic*. The psychic was Mary E. Matter and she claimed to channel the spirit of Ingersoll (1833–1899), the famed orator. As Matter held a pencil, "Ingersoll" supposedly guided it, thus writing about "the mansions far above" and other oratorical utterances. These had a somewhat literary quality, but did they represent the voice of Robert Green Ingersoll?

Actually, the questioned writing is unconvincing as the voice of Ingersoll, an atheist who seems unlikely to have used such biblical echoes (see Galatians 6:7). As a member of the International Association of Forensic Linguists, I decided to compare the questioned text with authentic Ingersoll writings. It soon became obvious that the supposedly channeled text has an overblown style with sentences that are too long and with too many polysyllabic words, among other significant differences. Tellingly, in contrast to the orator's genuine texts, the "Ingersoll" automatic writing has numerous grammatical errors, including noun-pronoun agreement errors, faulty verb-subject agreement, run-on sentences, faulty punctuation, and at least one misspelling. There is also faulty parallelism, among other writing faults. In short, linguistic analysis reveals that the questioned text is merely an imitation produced by the automatic writer—whether consciously or unconsciously (Nickell 2007b, 7).

Photographic Analysis

Photographs often show odd effects popularly attributed to ghosts or other supposedly paranormal causes. On Friday, October 27, 1995, the television program *Unsolved Mysteries* aired the segment "Kentucky Visions," which featured Polaroid photographs made by a Sunday school teacher who had visited the site of a recent Virgin Mary sighting near Bardstown, Kentucky. Among several "miracle" effects shown in the photos was one that often appeared in photos taken at such Marian apparition sites. Called the "golden door," this was an arched-door shape, flooded with golden light and supposed by some to be the doorway to heaven mentioned in the Bible (Revelation 4:1). Another effect consisted of bright streaks called "angel wings," and still another was a mysterious, unidentified *chart* superimposed on one picture—slightly out of focus but nevertheless unmistakable.

Members of the Georgia Skeptics group, Dale Heatherington and Anson Kennedy, had previously explained the "Golden Door" as an artifact of the Polaroid "OneStep" camera (which, when flooded with bright light, produces the shape of its own aperture), and they identified the "angel wings" effect as due to light leakage into the Polaroid film pack due to mishandling. In experimenting successfully to reproduce these, I discovered the cause of the chart effect. The chart proved to be the same as one printed on the underside of the protective card at the top of the pack. When light leaked between this card and the light-sensitive emulsion of the first photo, an exposure was made of a portion of the chart. In this way it was subsequently superimposed on the first photograph made from that pack. (See Nickell 2001, 174–178.)

Crime-Scene Reconstruction

On March 4, 1980, in Chorley, England, a woman's body was discovered severely destroyed by fire in her home, yet nearby surroundings were undamaged. Tony McMunn, a fireman who encountered the case and as a result became a proponent of "spontaneous human combustion," was impressed that the burning should have progressed so far and that some of the bones were even calcined (reduced to ash).

In fact, crime *reconstruction* (the attempt to ascertain the circumstances and sequence of events in a case [Nickell and Fischer 1999, 37–40]) easily resolved the mystery. Consider the following chronology, keyed to my pen-and-ink rendering of the crime scene (Figure 1, based on a published photo): (1) Bucket indicated to investigators that the victim, an elderly lady, was in the process of relieving herself when she fell. (2) The missing shoe is consistent with this or other possible scenarios. Apparently it came off during the fall—or her taking it off caused the fall—and is out of view. (3) In falling, the victim obviously hit her head on the fireplace, knocking her unconscious or possibly killing her outright. (4) Her head struck the iron grate, which has been sharply displaced to the left. (5) The fall caused flaming embers from the now-exposed "open coal fire" to shower upon the body. (6) The

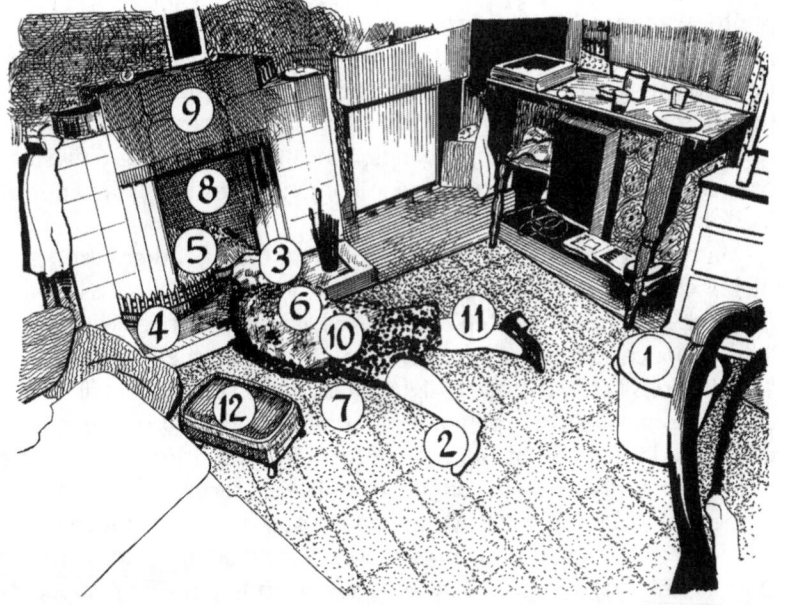

Figure 1. Reconstruction of a woman's death attributed by some to "Spontaneous Human Combustion" (drawing by Joe Nickell).

victim's clothing ignited and, as the fire progressed, her own melting body fat contributed to the overall destruction. (7) The rug beneath the body may have retained melted body fat to aid in the severe destruction—a process known in the forensic literature as the wick effect. (8) The fire was probably further aided by the chimney effect—a "drawing" of the flame and venting of smoke—in this case by the chimney itself. At about 9:30 on the previous evening, when it is believed the fire took place, neighbors saw a great amount of smoke and sparks issuing from the chimney. (9) Heavy deposits of soot above the fireplace, tapering toward the chimney opening, are consistent with the chimney effect and the venting of considerable organic material. (10) The destruction of the body was in approximate proportion to its proximity to the fire source, the torso—which contains a large amount of fat—being most severely destroyed, while the lower legs and feet have remained intact. (11) As in many other such cases, the lower extremities were spared because fire burns laterally with difficulty. (12) Nearby objects failed to burn for the same reason. Only radiant heat, and not flame, reached these objects. (See Nickell 2004, 162–164.)

Psychological Autopsy

In his collection of horror and mystery tales, Can Such Things Be? (1893), Ambrose Bierce included a trilogy of tales dubbed "Mysterious Disappearances." These have elements of the bizarre, and some have seen parallels with Bierce's own unsolved disappearance in late 1913. Theories abound—that he was killed in Mexico by Pancho Villa's forces or by those of the opposing side; that he secretly relocated to France; that he ended his days in an insane asylum; even that his disappearance was due to supernatural forces.

Actually, a "psychological autopsy"—the investigation of a decedent's mental state prior to death (Nickell and Fischer 1999, 255)—indicates the most likely scenario. Bierce had advocated suicide in a powerful essay on the subject. At age 72, tired and ill, he wrote letters to friends saying "My work is finished, and so am I," along with many similar sentiments. He showed his friend and publisher, Walter Neale, a photo of a place in the canyon of the Colorado which, says Neale, was to be "the place of his last earthly habitat," and Bierce said he had a German pistol for that purpose. He permanently closed out his affairs. He wrote his daughter that he was giving up his cemetery plot, saying he did "not wish to lie there. That matter is all arranged and you will not be bothered about the mortal part of [signed] Your Daddy."

(See Nickell with Fischer 1992, 19–34.) Bierce's biographer, Roy Morris Jr. (1995, 255–256, 263), referring to me as "a modern forensic investigator," finds this suicide scenario "hard to resist."

Profiling

The 1912 Piltdown forgery—the creation of a bogus "missing link" from stained human cranial fragments and an orangutan jawbone—has been regarded as the greatest hoax perpetrated in the name of science. The fragments were recovered from a gravel pit near Piltdown Common in Sussex, England, by Charles Dawson, an amateur fossil collector. However, others have been suspected of the *Eoanthropus dawsoni* hoax, including a young Jesuit priest named Teillard de Chardin, anatomists Sir Grafton Elliott Smith and Sir Arthur Keith, paleontologist William J. Solas, and several others, including even the likes of Sir Arthur Conan Doyle, the creator of Sherlock Holmes.

"Profiling" in such a case may be helpful—if by this we mean not the near-psychic process often portrayed in fiction but simply "educated guesswork based on crime scene evidence and statistical probability" (Newton 2008, 220). As it happens only one person was present at the recovery of each Piltdown fragment, as well as the recovery of a second set of bones (known as "Piltdown II"). This same individual was a knowledgeable amateur who is known to have inquired how to stain bones to make them appear ancient and had part of yet another stained skull (Piltdown III?) in his possession at his death. And—in contrast to many other "suspects" who were reputable men—he had not only been accused of plagiarism but had to his credit *several other bogus finds*. This man was Charles Dawson. He had written in a letter in 1909 that he was "waiting for the big discovery which never seems to come"; and then came the Piltdown "discovery." (See Nickell with Fischer 1992, 131–143.)

* * *

As the foregoing examples demonstrate, forensic sciences can be valuable resources for the paranormal investigator, who will do well to become familiar with the different disciplines and consider how one or another might be applied to solve some intriguing mystery.

Fauxrensics: Pseudoscience vs. Forensic Science

As coauthor of a forensic textbook, *Crime Science* (Nickell and Fischer 1999), I have often witnessed the abuses of crime pseudoscience, or what I call fauxrensics. The term incorporates approaches that some would hope to include with forensic science but are at best problematic. While some fields are entirely pseudoscientific, others may be only partially so, and even perfectly scientific disciples can be misused in a pseudoscientific way.[1] Here is an investigative look at several examples.

Early Pseudosciences

In earlier times, especially, pseudoscience often masqueraded as science. Consider, for example, *cranioscopy*, an alleged means of determining a person's intelligence level, personality, and moral development—all of interest to the criminologist. This was proposed by German neuro-anatomist Franz Gall (1758–1828) and depended on the shape of the subject's skull. Cranioscopy was opposed by the Catholic Church on the grounds that it challenged the divine basis of the human mind, and it was dismissed as well in France, Gall having moved there in 1805, when the Institute of France ruled the claims invalid. Gall's colleague Johann Spurzheim renamed the pseudoscience *phrenology*, and it went on to flourish for a time in Britain and even longer in the United States. Nevertheless, years after Gall's death in 1828, some of his theories on the localization of brain function came to be validated, helping to lay some of the groundwork for forensic psychiatry (Newton 2008, 119).

Like phrenology, physiognomy—the attempted divining of character from facial features—raised the question: Was it the targeted individual or the supposed scientist who ought to have his head examined? From

1870, one Cesare Lombroso aimed to identify the criminal "type" by indexing the facial characteristics of imprisoned criminals, based on an international collection of some 4,000 photos (Frizot 1998, 264–267). He concluded, "we can now ascertain—with ease, simply by holding up a photograph—that among criminal men the predominant features are a massively developed jaw, sparse beard, hard eyes, thick hair and, secondarily, sticking-out ears, receding brow, a squint, and a misshapen nose" (qtd. in Frizot 1998, 266). It all seems laughable in retrospect.

No less a personage than Darwin's cousin Sir Francis Galton (1822–1911)—who made important contributions to fingerprinting and numerous other fields—was lured into physiognomy's pseudoscientific sphere. Galton devised a means of "composite photography" (in itself an interesting development), by which he proposed identifying a variety of human "types"—criminals among them—simply by their appearance (Newton 2008, 119–120). By the end of the century, physiognomy was no longer influential to the scientific community, although in the late 1930s it was turned into a "science" called "personology" by one Edward Vincent Jones, a California judge. He claimed he could look at criminals' features and guess the crimes they were accused of—never under scientifically controlled conditions, of course (Justice 1997, 4; "What" 2010).

Another pseudoscientific notion—belief in "spontaneous human combustion" (SHC)—had significant implications to western jurisprudence in the eighteenth and nineteenth centuries. Interestingly, the concept was used in some instances to clear people wrongly suspected of murder! From at least the eighteenth century came baffling burning deaths, in which a lack of apparent cause for the ignition, coupled with often bizarre destruction of the body, led some detectives and prosecutors to suspect foul play, while some pathologists cited SHC as a more likely explanation. The alleged phenomenon was promoted by the temperance movement, on the grounds that excessive imbibing of alcohol might heighten the body's flammability, and Charles Dickens killed off a drunken character by SHC in his novel *Bleak House*.

In fact, one would die of alcohol poisoning before achieving even a slight effect on the body's flammability. As the great scientist Liebig (1851) wrote with scientific clarity, "The opinion that a man can burn of himself is not founded on a knowledge of the circumstances of the death, but on the reverse of knowledge—on complete ignorance of all the causes or conditions which preceded the accident and caused it." That is, SHC is promoted by the logical fallacy called arguing from ignorance (i.e., "we don't know what causes a given fiery death, so it must have been SHC"). Forensic analyst John F. Fischer and I conducted a two-year investigation of thirty historical cases of the alleged phenomenon and found that there were invariably plausible causes for the ignition. In cases of extreme bodily destruction, the victim's own melting body fat appeared to play a role, being absorbed by clothing, chair stuffing, carpeting, or the like to fuel still more fire to burn still more of the body efficiently—a cyclic phenomenon known as the wick or candle effect (Nickell with Fischer 1988, 149–157, 161–171).

Two of the cases we investigated—both French, one of an alcoholic woman in 1725, the other of an elderly man in 1847—were initially classed as homicide. However, the convicted husband in the first instance, and the accused son and daughter-in-law in the second, were freed after the deaths were attributed to spontaneous combustion. Although unscientific, the determinations had the desirable result of sparing probably innocent people in cases that today would likely be recognized as accidents caused by carelessness with fire (Nickell with Fischer 1988, 161, 163). Belief in SHC continues (Arnold 1995), but fire and arson investigators are increasingly becoming informed and adopting the scientific view.[2]

Graphology

It appears to have been the ancient Jews who first recognized the individuality inherent in handwriting, a recognition codified in the Mishnah in the first and second centuries. It is today a basic principle of forensic handwriting comparison (Nickell 1996, 17–53). Unfortunately, the individuality has also served as the basis of another type of "handwriting analysis" called *graphology* (from Greek words for *writing* and *doctrine*). Apparently practiced by the Romans (Nero supposedly distrusted a man because "his handwriting showed him treacherous") and by the Chinese as early as the eleventh century, graphology was developed in seventeenth-century Italy. There a physician named Camillo Baldi explicated the perceived relationship between handwriting and personality, prompting some itinerant magicians to go from castle to castle giving graphological readings (Nickell 1996, 17–18).

Modern graphology was spread by a particular circle of French clerics beginning in the 1830s. Abbé Jean-Hippolyte Michon (1806–1881) established the term *graphology* and attempted to make it a science by associating isolated "signs" (such as flourishes, *i*-dots, and *t*-bars) with particular character traits (Nickell 1996, 18). However, as Martin

Gardner (1957, 296–297) observes in his classic skeptical treatise, *Fads and Fallacies in the Name of Science*:

> One of the major difficulties in all forms of character reading research is that no really precise methods have yet been devised for determining whether an analysis fits the person or not. Wide margins on a written letter, for example, are supposed to indicate "generosity." Is there anyone who would not feel that such a trait applied to himself? People are generous in some ways and not in others. It is too vague a trait to be tested by empirical method, and even good friends may disagree widely on whether it applies to a given individual. The same is true of most of the graphological traits. If you are told you have them, you can always look deep enough and find them—especially if you are convinced that the graphologist who made the analysis is an expert who is seldom wrong.

Most of the empirical studies of graphology fail to demonstrate the validity its supporters claim. This confirms the wisdom of British expert Wilson R. Harrison who predicted, in his forensic textbook *Suspect Documents* (1958, 518–519), "It is unlikely that graphology will ever be raised to the status of an experimental science. . . ."

Nevertheless, graphologists purport to be able to foresee juvenile delinquency by examining children's handwriting and to detect potential pilferers and other miscreants from the script of employees and job applicants (Holder 1969, 119–123, 130–138). Other alarming legal applications include proposed jury screening, in which a graphologist would examine perspective jurors' handwriting to determine who should be excluded based on their purported personality profile ("Graphology" 2010). (For further discussion, see Beyerstein and Beyerstein, *The Write Stuff: Evaluations of Graphology* [1992], including two chapters that I contributed.)

Police Psychics

Even though mainstream science has never validated any psychic ability, self-styled clairvoyants, spirit mediums, soothsayers, and diviners of various stripes, including astrologers and tarot card readers, continue to try to insinuate themselves in criminal investigations. An example was the case of the Atlanta Child Murders in which, over a twenty-two-month period beginning in July 1979, thirty African American children and young men disappeared or were found murdered. The serial killings made national and international headlines. In time, forensic and other evidence led to the arrest and conviction of a young black man named Wayne Williams. Much of the evidence against

Williams involved powerful, cutting-edge forensic fiber analysis, and I was able to discuss the case at a forensic microscopy conference with the analyst who did this trace-evidence examination, Larry Peterson. I wrote an account of the case for my book *Crime Science* (Nickell and Fischer 1999, 75–84).

At the time of the murders, however, a circus atmosphere often prevailed. Along with Williams' own bold, defiant antics, "psychics were swarming around . . . many dramatically contradicting each other" (Douglas and Olshaker 1995, 211). The clairvoyants were of no help to police whatsoever; in fact, they were a serious nuisance. Among them was self-styled "police psychic" Dorothy Allison, who claimed she had given police the serial killer's name. In fact, "she provided police with 42 different names, none of which was Wayne or Williams" (Rowe 1993, 238). Moreover, Allison's prophecy "that a major break in the case would occur on 12 November also proved wrong," according to *Science* magazine, which concluded, "In Atlanta on her biggest consulting job so far, she proved a flop" (Marshall 1980, 994).

Again, consider the case of Chandra Levy, the Washington intern whose 2001 disappearance garnered widespread media attention and also served as a magnet for psychics. During more than a year of media focus on the missing young woman, at every opportunity I challenged the psychic community to tell us where Chandra was and not merely play their old game of *retrofitting*. That technique involves throwing out vague clues like "water" or "the number seven" and then attempting to match them with the facts once they are known. (See my *Psychic Sleuths* [Nickell 1994].)

Nevertheless, Levy's romantic affair with Representative Gary Condit and the publicized fact of her having looked up a park site on her computer on the day of her disappearance led some prognosticators to "see" her still in the park, or to believe, with James van Pragh, that she had been tricked into a car with the promise that she "was going to Condit's." Another felt she was alive, possibly in a Brookline apartment, while Sylvia Browne envisioned her "down in a marshy area." And so on. Actually, Levy's remains were on a steep, wooded slope in the park. A dog on a morning outing with its owner sniffed at a site, and when the man swept away debris he discovered a skull and alerted authorities (Nickell 2009). Once again "psychics" proved no more than a distraction.

Psychics sometimes use a simpler technique than retrofitting: they make utterly false claims, such as with a case I investigated after appearing with alleged visionary Ron Bard on the *Mark Wallberg Show* on

February 7, 1996. Bard claimed, "I've solved over 110 murder cases and returned 150 missing children in my career so far." He stated that "The one that stands in my mind most was two girls found in plastic bags in Harrison, New York." Bard went on to claim that he had taken a key from one of the dead girls' bodies, which led him to the south Bronx, and "the key worked in the lock and that's how we found the murderer." Bard added, "Anybody can call the chief of Harrison Police Department and find this out for fact." I resolved to do just that. Unfortunately, Chief Louis Dorio explained to me that no key had led to the discovery of the murderer. Neither was Bard even involved in the case, although his *mother* had made certain pronouncements that were of no assistance. In fact, said Chief Dorio, "Our arrest and convictions were due to diligent police work, not visions." And this was supposed to be one of Bard's most outstanding successes (Nickell 2001, 210–213).

Despite such failures, psychics thrive, playing to an often gullible public and lazy news media. A study conducted by Martin Reiser, director of the Behavioral Science Services Section of the Los Angeles Police Department, together with several associates, concluded: "The research data do not support the contention that psychics can provide significant additional information leading to the solution of major crimes." Therefore, "We are forced to conclude, based on our results, that the usefulness of psychics as an aid in criminal investigation has not been validated" (Reiser et al. 1979, 197).

Fauxrensic Serology

Among forensic specialties, *serology*, the science that studies the properties and effects of serums, often plays a crucial role in investigations. It encompasses blood, saliva, semen, perspiration, and even fecal matter. However, forensic serology stands in contrast to its pseudoscientific lookalike, both of which have played roles in the investigation of the notorious Shroud of Turin, alleged to be Jesus's burial linen. As might be expected, the approaches have yielded dramatically different results.

A secret commission was appointed in 1973 to study the cloth's image and "blood" stains. The team included internationally known forensic serologists. Even though the supposed blood was suspiciously still distinctly red (unlike old blood that blackens with age) and appeared on the cloth in a "picturelike" fashion (instead of soaking and spreading into the cloth), the experts excised several threads and conducted a battery of tests. These included microscopical, chemical, biological, and instrumental tests. Not only were all of these negative, but reddish granules on the threads would not even dissolve in reagents that dissolve blood, and one investigator found traces of what appeared to be paint. Later tests by distinguished microanalyst Walter McCrone found that the "blood" actually consisted of red ocher and vermilion tempera paint (Nickell 1998, 127–132).

Undeterred, a pro-shroud group, whose leaders served on the executive council of the Holy Shroud Guild, gave samples to two scientists—neither being a forensic serologist or a pigment expert. One admitted that McCrone "had over two decades of experience with this kind of problem and a worldwide reputation," while the two of them "had never before tackled anything like an artistic forgery" (Heller 1983, 168). Nevertheless, they soon proclaimed they had identified the presence of blood on the shroud samples. However, at the 1983 conference of the prestigious International Association for Identification, forensic analyst John F. Fischer explained how results similar to theirs could have been obtained from tempera paint. They had used a forensically invalid method to supposedly identify blood—a this-plus-this approach. But blood is not identified by adding together positive results for the presence of iron, protein, and so on, especially since a red ocher (iron oxide) tempera paint would also test positive for these substances. Crucially, not a single test conducted by the two scientists was specific for blood, in contrast to the tests conducted by the secret commission's forensic serologists, which yielded consistently negative results (Fischer 1983). Another non-serologist Shroud proponent has more recently found the tempera paint to be type AB blood! But even other shroud advocates have called such claims nonsense (Nickell 2007, 176).

Nonsense describes much of what I call "shroud science." In contrast to real science, its adherents begin with the desired answer, then work backward to the evidence, picking and choosing to support their prior belief. The scientific approach instead is to seek accurate evidence, let that lead to the probable answer, and provisionally believe that—like it or not. (In this instance, the evidence—including radiocarbon dating—shows that the shroud was produced in the mid-fourteenth century, at which time, a bishop reported, an artist confessed it was his handiwork [Nickell 1998].)

Other Forensic Techniques

Many other examples of crime pseudoscience could be included, although some techniques represent more complex issues than those discussed here. Among such techniques are the varieties of supposed lie detection (see, e.g., Shneour 1990; Zelicoff 2001; Frazier 2007), psychological profiling (Newton 2008, 220–222), and hypnosis (Baker 1990)—not all being totally useless but all requiring extreme caution and needing to be limited to investigative rather than trial use.

In law as in medicine, where life-and-death matters are engaged, one understands the proven worth of the scientific method. Pseudoscience, which sets science on its head, is an abomination (Hines 1988). It should be relegated to the proverbial dustbin of history—though not, perhaps, until we have looked over it with our magnifying glass to attempt to see in it, and in ourselves, why it so often continues to deceive.

Notes

1. For a discussion of how legal systems can affect science and pseudoscience, see John E. Dodes (2001), "Junk Science and the Law."

2. On November 5, 2010, I lectured on the topic at an arson investigators training program at the Academy of Fire Science in Montour Falls, New York.

References

Anson, Jay. 1977. *The Amityville Horror.* New York: Bantam Books.

Arnold, Larry E. 1995. *Ablaze! The Mysterious Fires of Spontaneous Human Combustion.* New York: M. Evans and Co.

Baker, Robert A. 1990. *They Call It Hypnosis.* Buffalo, N.Y.: Prometheus Books. (See especially the discussion of forensic hypnosis, 262–267.)

Baker, Robert A. 1992. *Hidden Memories: Voices and Visions from Within.* Buffalo, N.Y.: Prometheus Books.

Baker, Robert A., and Joe Nickell. 1992. *Missing Pieces: How to Investigate Ghosts, UFOs, Psychics, and other Mysteries.* Buffalo, N.Y.: Prometheus Books.

Beveridge, W.I.B. n.d. *The Art of Scientific Investigation.* New York: Vintage.

Beyerstein, Barry L., and Dale F. Beyerstein. 1992. *The Write Stuff: Evaluations of Graphology.* Buffalo, N.Y.: Prometheus Books.

The big picture. 1983. *Scientific American* June, 84.

Bilger, Burkhard. 2002. Waiting for ghosts. *New Yorker,* Dec. 23 and 30, 86–100.

Binder, David A., and Paul Bergman. 1984. *Fact Investigation: From Hypothesis to Proof.* St. Paul: West.

Christopher, Milbourne. 1970. *ESP, Seers & Psychics: What the Occult Really Is.* New York: Thomas Y. Crowell.

Dodes, John E. 2001. Junk science and the law. *Skeptical Inquirer.* 25:4 (July/August), 31–34.

Douglas, John, and Mark Olshaker. 1995. *Mind Hunter: Inside the FBI's Elite Serial Crimes Unit.* New York: Scribner's.

Fischer, John F. 1983. A summary critique of analyses of the "blood" on the Turin "shroud." In Nickell 1998, 155–158.

Frazier, Kendrick. 2007. *Skeptical Inquirer.* 31:1 (January/February), 8.

Frizot, Michael, ed. 1998. *A New History of Photography.* N.p.: Konemann.

Gardner, Martin. 1957. *Fads and Fallacies in the Name of Science.* New York: Dover.

Graphology. 2010. Available online at http://en.wikipedia.org/wiki/Graphology; accessed March 8, 2010.

Harrison, Wilson R. 1958. *Suspect Documents: Their Scientific Evaluation.* New York: Frederick A. Praeger.

Hart, Brian. 2006. Carla Baron, psychic detective? Not quite. *Skeptical Inquirer* 30:5 (September/October), 5.

Heller, John. 1983. *Report on the Shroud of Turin*. New York: Houghton Mifflin.

Hill, Myron G. Jr., et al. 1978. *Evidence*. St. Paul: West.

Hines, Terence. 1988. *Pseudoscience and the Paranormal*. Amherst, N.Y.: Prometheus Books.

Holder, Robert. 1969. *You Can Analyze Handwriting*. New York: Signet.

Houdini, Harry. 1924. *A Magician Among the Spirits*. New York: Harper & Brothers.

Justice, L.A. 1997. *How to Read Faces!* Boca Raton, Florida: Globe Communications.

Kalush, William, and Larry Sloman. 2006. *The Secret Life of Houdini*. New York: Atria Books.

Keene, M. Lamar. 1976. *The Psychic Mafia*. Amherst, N.Y.: Prometheus Books.

Kurtz, Paul. 1994. *Toward a New Enlightenment: The Philosophy of Paul Kurtz*, ed. by Vern L. Bullough and Timothy J. Madigan. London: Transaction.

Liebig, Justus von. 1851. *Familiar Letters on Chemistry*, letter no. 22. London: Taylor, Walton & Maberly.

Marshall, Eliot. 1980. Police, science and psychics. *Science*. November 28: 994.

Morris, Roy Jr. 1995. *Ambrose Bierce: Alone in Bad Company*. New York: Crown Publishers.

Newton, Michael. 2008. *The Encyclopedia of Crime Scene Investigation*. New York: Checkmark Books.

Nickell, Joe. 1989. *The Magic Detectives*. Buffalo, N.Y.: Prometheus Books.

———. 1995. *Entities: Angels, Spirits, Demons, and Other Alien Beings*. Amherst, N.Y.: Prometheus Books.

———. 1996. *Detecting Forgery: Forensic Investigation of Documents*. Lexington, Ky.: University Press of Kentucky.

———. 1998. *Inquest on the Shroud of Turin*. Amherst, N.Y.: Prometheus Books.

———. 2001. *Real-Life X-Files*. Lexington, Ky.: University Press of Kentucky.

———. 2004. *The Mystery Chronicles: More Real-Life X-Files*. Lexington, Ky.: University Press of Kentucky.

———. 2006. Ghost hunters. *Skeptical Inquirer* 30:5 (September/October), 23–26.

———. 2007. *Relics of the Christ*. Lexington, Ky.: University Press of Kentucky.

———. 2007a. *Adventures in Paranormal Investigation*. Lexington, Ky.: University Press of Kentucky.

———. 2007b. A case of automatic writing. *Skeptical Briefs* 17:4 (December), 5–7.

———. 2007c. Lake monster lookalikes. *Skeptical Briefs* 17:2 (June), 6–7.

———. 2007d. Peru's ancient mysteries. *Skeptical Inquirer* 31:4 (July/August) 15–19.

———. 2009. Levy case a psychic failure. *Investigative Briefs*. Available online at http://www.centerforinquiry.net/blogs/show/levy_case_a_psychic-failure/; accessed March 8, 2010.

Nickell, Joe, ed. 1994. *Psychic Sleuths*. Buffalo, N.Y.: Prometheus Books.

Nickell, Joe, with John F. Fischer. 1988. *Secrets of the Supernatural: Investigating the World's Occult Mysteries*. Amherst, N.Y.: Prometheus Books.

Nickell, Joe, with John F. Fischer. 1992. *Mysterious Realms: Probing Paranormal Historical and Forensic Enigmas*. Buffalo, N.Y.: Prometheus Books.

Nickell, Joe, and John F. Fischer. 1999. *Crime Science: Methods of Forensic Detection*. Lexington, Ky.: University Press of Kentucky.

Price, Harry. 1936. *Confessions of a Ghost Hunter*. London: Putnam.

Randi, James. 1987. *The Faith Healers*. Buffalo, N.Y.: Prometheus Books.

Reiser, Martin, et al. 1979. An evaluation of the use of psychics in the investigation of major crimes. Appendix A of Nickell 1994, 193–203.

Rowe, Walter F. 1993. Psychic detectives: A critical examination. Reprinted in Nickell

1994, 236–244.

Shneour, Elie. A. 1986. Occam's razor. *Skeptical Inquirer* 10:4 (Summer), 310–313.

———. 1990. Lying about polygraph tests. *Skeptical Inquirer* 14:3 (Spring), 292–297.

Steiner, Robert. 1986. Exposing the faith-healers. *Skeptical Inquirer* 11:1 (Fall), 28–31.

———. 1989. *Don't Get Taken*. El Cerrito, CA: Wide-Awake Books.

What Is personology? 2010. Available online at http://personology.com/what/; accessed March 5, 2010.

Zelicoff, Alan P. 2001. Polygraphs and the national labs: Dangerous ruse undermines national security. *Skeptical Inquirer* 25:4 (July/August), 21–23.

CASE
STUDIES

Quest for the Giant Eel

On a six-day trip to the Canadian province of Newfoundland and Labrador (in part for a television documentary), I encountered some very large creatures: several moose (the largest land mammal of the region), to whom I gave the right of way in return for their photos; a stuffed polar bear (towering upright almost nine feet tall), which had ambled into St. Anthony one spring; and, from a circus truck that overturned ahead of me on the Viking Trail, two camels and a sweet Asian elephant named Limba.

I did not encounter humpback whales, although I took an excursion boat out in very rough water to see great icebergs making their way south from Greenland. (I had better luck with humpbacks on an Alaska excursion [Nickell 2007a].) Neither did I catch a glimpse of another leviathan that occasionally haunts the region's coastal waters: the giant squid, known at lengths in excess of seventy-five feet and the subject of numerous hair-raising adventures (Fitzgerald 2006, 50–71). (For our book *Lake Monster Mysteries*, Benjamin Radford [2006, 5] photographed the world's best-preserved specimen at a museum in St. John's.)

What I was really searching for—having been brought to the village of Robert's Arm by a television crew for the History Channel's popular series, *Monster Quest* (which later aired on September 17, 2008)—was a legendary lake monster said to inhabit the cold, deep, blue waters of Crescent Lake. It has been dubbed "Cressie," and the village's welcoming signboard proclaims it "The 'Loch Ness' of Newfoundland!"

'Cressie'

Sightings of a "monster" in the lake date back to the turn of the last century when a resident known as "Grandmother Anthony" spied a giant serpen-

59

tine creature while she was picking berries. From the 1940s to the present, there have been a dozen or so sightings, although without photographs to date. Most descriptions are of a dark eel-like creature, up to twenty-five or more feet long (Bragg 1995; Radford and Nickell 2006, 89–95).

Its locomotion is typically described as "rolling" or "undulating" (Bragg 1995); indeed, "when the head was up, the back was down" (Colbourne 2008). Consequently, the contortions of the elongated creature seemingly produced "humps" (Short 2008; see Figure 1).

A typical sighting occurred in 1991, when retired school teacher Fred Parsons (an engaging man whom I met in Robert's Arm) saw a creature surface while crossing the lake. It was dark brown, swimming in an undulating fashion, and, Parsons estimated, over twenty feet long (Bragg 1995; see also Radford and Nickell 2006, 92–93). Of course eyewitness testimony can be unreliable. An experiment I conducted for *Monster Quest*, using a log of known length that we towed and anchored at a mid-lake position, demonstrated that people viewing something from a distance can easily overestimate its size by forty percent or greater.[1]

There are other reasons to be skeptical of a monster in Crescent Lake, one of which is that a single creature could neither live for cen-

Figure 1. For the TV series *Monster Quest*, the author visited Crescent Lake, Newfoundland, where "Cressie" is reported to lurk—possibly as a giant eel.

turies nor reproduce itself. A breeding herd of several individuals would be required for the species to continue propagating over time. But then where is a single floating or beached carcass? It is true that the lake is connected to the Atlantic Ocean, scarcely two miles distant, by Tommy's Arm Brook. However as Bragg (1995) concedes, no great creature has ever been seen navigating the outlet.

Giant Eel?

Because "Cressie" is often likened to a giant eel (Bragg 1995; Eberhart 2002, I:114; *Monster* 2008), someone gave it the quasi-scientific name *Cressiteras anguilloida* (Eberhart 2002, I:114). Actually, this is unlikely as a scientific name that might be bestowed—if a giant-eel specimen were verified. Eels (a group of fishes having snakelike bodies and lacking pelvic fins) are of the order *Anguilliformes*, and true eels compose the family *Anguillidae*. The American eel, for example, is *Anguilla rostrata* (Collins 1959, 475). Related eels include the marine conger eels (*Conger oceanicus*), which attain a length of six to nine feet, and the morays of tropical reefs. The Pacific moray (*Thyrsoidea macrurus*), up to a foot longer, "is probably the largest known species" (*Colliers Encyclopedia* 1993, s.v. "Moray").

Now, while Crescent Lake does reportedly host freshwater American eels, these are normally under five feet long. Divers from the Royal Canadian Mounted Police (RCMP), who allegedly surfaced on the lake with "descriptions of giant eels as thick as a man's thigh" (Bragg 1995), probably encountered a different creature—if indeed, the incident actually happened: The RCMP could not confirm the occurrence to *Monster Quest*. Indeed, whatever Cressie is, it is clearly not a giant eel. The eyewitness descriptions of a giant creature, swimming on the surface of the water and moving in an up-and-down fashion, are completely wrong for an eel.

Eels, in fact, are bottom-dwelling creatures ("Freshwater" 2008a, 2008b; "Eel" 2008), and their locomotion, while wavelike, is actually from side-to-side, as I confirmed by studying them at Aquarium Niagara in Niagara Falls, New York (where I am a member and once served as "Animal Trainer for a Day"). For my *Monster Quest* research, the aquarium's exhibits supervisor, Dan Arcara, graciously allowed me to study an American eel and a moray eel, gently prodding the latter from its den with a pole so I could document on videotape its sideways-oscillating swimming style.

Moreover, the sightings of Cressie invariably occur during daytime, whereas the common freshwater eel "is nocturnal in its habits, sleeping or lying in the mud during the day" ("Freshwater" 2008a).

Cressie Lookalike

There is, in fact, an actual creature that is dark-colored, swims both under water and at the surface—where its wake can make it appear much longer, and moves in an undulating (rising and falling) manner. Its scientific name is *Lontra canadensis*,[2] the northern river otter (Nickell 2007c).

In addition, multiple otters swimming in a line can give the effect of a single giant serpentine creature slithering with an up-and-down movement through water. This effect was observed as early as 1930 by a marine biologist (Gould 1934, 115–116) and has since been documented many times (e.g., Nickell 2007b). Newfoundland is shown (by the *National Audubon Society Field Guide to Mammals* [Whitaker 1996, 782–785]) to be a definite habitat for the northern river otter. (See Figure 2.)

I have been accused of seeming to suggest this effect as a solution to all lake monster reports (Coleman 2007), but in fact that grossly mischaracterizes my position. In *Lake Monster Mysteries*, I acknowledged other lake-monster imitators, including fish (such as sturgeon and gar), long-necked birds, windslicks, boat wakes, and logs (which may be propelled from the lake bottom by methane gas produced by decomposition [Monk 2004]). Swimming mammals like deer and beaver have also

Figure 2. Giant eel or otter lookalike?

been mistaken for lake monsters. For instance, during the filming of the *Monster Quest* program, a mysterious and seemingly lengthy creature swimming under the surface of the lake created a brief sensation but proved to be a beaver.

I apply otters as a solution to *some* mystery sightings, according to the principle of Occam's razor (that the simplest credible solution, the one making the fewest assumptions, is to be preferred). When a sighting could most credibly be explained as one or more otters, like some of the Cressie sightings, then that is necessarily the preferred hypothesis. Other sightings may be attributed to other causes. However, should Cressie surface in a more credible form, I would certainly be willing to reopen the case.

Acknowledgments

In addition to those mentioned in the text, I wish to thank the residents of Robert's Arm, Newfoundland, who generously hosted a reception for the *Monster Quest* crew and me, complete with a wonderful seafood dinner and ceremony naming each of us an "Honorary Newfoundlander."

I also wish to thank CMJ Productions—including producer Leo Singer, production staffer Saskia DeBoer, and the film crew, as well as CFI Libraries Director Timothy Binga for their help.

Notes

1. This was conducted on Saturday, June 14, 2008. Two of the three participants—Bradley Rideout (2008) and Effie Colbourne—had reported seeing "Cressie." Brad estimated the 14.25-foot log at 18 feet, Effie at 20 (although first saying "20 to 30"), and the other participant at 20 feet.

2. Formerly *Lutra canadensis*.

References

Bragg, R.A. 1995. Have you seen Cressie? In Wanda Jackman, Bonnie Warr, and Russell A. Bragg, *Remembrances of Robert's Arm*. Corner Brook, Newfoundland: Western Star Publishers, 14.

Colbourne, Effie. 2008. Interview for *Monster Quest* (*Monster* 2008).

Coleman, Loren. 2007. Otter nonsense. Available online at www.cryptomundo.com/cryptozoo-news/otter-nonsense; accessed June 6, 2007.

Collins, Henry Hill. 1959. *Complete Field Guide to American Wildlife*. New York: Harper.

Eberhart, George M. 2002. *Mysterious Creatures: A Guide to Cryptozoology* (in two vols.). Santa Barbara, Calif.: ABC-CL10.

Eel. 2008. From Wikipedia, available online at http://en.wikipedia.org/wiki/Eel; accessed August 20, 2008.

Fitzgerald, Jack. 2006. *Newfoundland Adventures: In Air, on Land, at Sea*. St. John's, Newfoundland and Labrador: Creative Publishers.

Freshwater eels. 2008a. Available online at http://gamefishingguide.com/freshwater-eels.html; accessed August 8, 2008.

Freshwater vs. saltwater moray eels revisited. 2008b. Available online at http://

Saltaquarium.about.com/cs/eelcare/a/aa090501.html; accessed August 20, 2008.

Gould, Rupert T. 1934. *The Loch Ness Monster*; reprinted Secaucus, N.J.: Citadel Press, 1976.

Monk, Jerry. 2004. Letter to the editor. *Fortean Times* 185 (July): 76.

Monster Quest eyewitnesses. 2008. Transcript of preliminary interviews for *Monster Quest*, provided to author September 6.

Nickell, Joe. 2007a. Mysterious entities of the Pacific Northwest, part I. *Skeptical Inquirer* 31:1 (January/February), 20–22.

———. 2007b. Lake monster lookalikes. *Skeptical Briefs*. June, 6–7.

———. 2007c. The Loch Ness critter. *Skeptical Inquirer* 31:5 (September/October), 15–16.

Radford, Benjamin, and Joe Nickell. 2006. *Lake Monster Mysteries: Investigating the World's Most Elusive Creatures*. Lexington, Ky.: The University Press of Kentucky.

Rideout, Bradley. 2008. Interview for *Monster Quest* (*Monster* 2008).

Short, Vivian. 2008. Interview for *Monster Quest* (*Monster* 2008).

Whitaker, John O., Jr. 1996. *National Audubon Society Field Guide to North American Mammals*. New York: Alfred A. Knopf.

Lighthouse Specters

Remote sentinels on rocky shores, lighthouses have been called "America's castles" (Hermanson n.d.). Certainly, they are places of scenic beauty, romance, and legend. From the late eighteenth century until the last lighthouse tower was automated in the 1960s, lighthouse keepers and their families worked around the clock at the lonely job of maintaining light stations—keeping the beacons lit and, when necessary, the fog signals sounding. If many popular writers are to be believed, the spirits of some keepers, shipwreck victims, and others still maintain their lonely vigils (Elizabeth 1999, vii; Thompson 1998, 7).

Investigating On Site

Over the years I have visited and investigated many of these "haunted" sites. I climbed the 219 steps of the 165-foot lighthouse at St. Augustine, Florida. As "assistant keepers," my wife and I stayed a few days in the remote Big Bay Point Lighthouse on Michigan's upper Peninsula perched on a cliff overlooking Lake Superior. We did the same at Thirty Mile Point Light on Lake Ontario (so named because it is thirty miles east of the mouth of the Niagara River). A bonus of the latter was access to a few years of entries recorded in its guest books—or maybe I should say ghost books given the various mentions, pro and con, of spooky phenomena.

In addition, I have visited other reputedly haunted sites, such as Lake Michigan's Seul Choix Point Lighthouse (Figure 1) (escorted up to the lantern room by Coast Guard maintenance men); the "French Castle" (officers quarters) at Old Fort Niagara, which had a navigational light placed atop it in 1780 (Grant and Jones 2002, 112–113); and the old and new lighthouses at Presque Isle, Michigan, on Lake Huron; as well as other lighthouses and proximate coastal areas.

Figure 1. The author and his wife (Diana G. Harris) picnic at "haunted" Seul Choix Point Lighthouse on Lake Michigan (watercolor sketch by Joe Nickell).

At some of the sites—such as Peggy's Cove, Nova Scotia, and Cape Hattaras and Ocracoke, North Carolina—ghosts are not reported in the lighthouses per se but rather are experienced as apparitions seen along the nearby seashore.

Apparitions

Among apparitional experiences—which involve the supposed sensing of a dead person (by sound, scent, or even touch)—a minority are visual sightings (Guiley 2000, 16). For example, as with supposedly haunted inns, some historic lighthouses and keepers' cottages have overnight guests who may awaken to see a spectral figure. Such was the case with intrepid lighthouse photographers Bob and Sandra Shanklin, who were able to spend a night at Plymouth Bay, Massachusetts. According to Bob: "I saw a woman's face hovering about fifteen or sixteen inches above Sandra's face. She had a blue-green, iridescent appearance, and she was wearing an old-timey garment that buttoned tight around her long neck." When he looked away for a moment, she vanished. "I hate that I didn't wake up Sandra, so she could see her, too," he added.

Given the woman's quaint dress, the Shanklins thought she might have been the ghost of Hannah Thomas. Hannah had carried on the duties of her husband John while he served in the Revolutionary War and for a period following, when he failed to return and was presumed dead. In 1790, officials made her the first designated female lighthouse keeper in America (Elizabeth and Roberts 1999, 15–21).

The report of another spectral sighting comes from Big Bay Point Lighthouse. Several years ago, a lady saw "a man in a beard and hat" standing at the foot of her bed. The credulous believe he was the "restless spirit" of former lighthouse keeper William Prior who—despondent over the death of his son—hanged himself in the woods in 1901 (Stonehouse 1997, 32).

Actually, however, neurologists and psychologists attribute such "ghost" sightings to a type of dream that occurs in the twilight between sleep and wakefulness. Called "waking dreams" (known in earlier times as "night terrors"), they are quite common and are very realistic to those who experience them (Nickell 1995, 41, 117).

But what about apparitions that are seen during normal waking activity? My own investigative experience, as well as other research data, demonstrates that apparitions are most likely to be perceived during daydreams or other altered states of consciousness. Many occur, for example, while the experiencer is in a relaxed state or concentrating on some activity like reading or performing routine work. Under such conditions, particularly in the case of imaginative persons, a mental image might emerge from the subconscious and be briefly superimposed on the visual scene, yielding a "sighting" (Nickell 2001, 291–292). Researcher G.N.M. Tyrrell (1973) noted that apparitions of people appear fully clothed and are often accompanied by objects, just as they are in dreams, because the clothes and objects are required by the apparitional drama.

Such mental images may be the basis for sightings of figures like the "Lady in Blue," who has allegedly been seen over the years near the lighthouse at Peggy's Cove, Nova Scotia ("Peggy's Cove" 2008a, 2008b); the "girl wearing a red dress" in the keepers' dwelling at St. Augustine Lighthouse (Elizabeth and Roberts 1999, 41–45); the apparition of a shipwrecked "old salt" at Ram Island Light in Boothbay Harbor, Maine (Thompson 1998, 71); or the figure of Aaron Burr's daughter, Theodosia, on the beach near Cape Hattaras Lighthouse (or is it the lighthouse on Ocracoke Island?) (Elizabeth and Roberts 1999, 65–73; Elizabeth and Roberts 2004, 9, 11; Zepke 1999, 78–81). In any event, all of these sightings are accompanied by multiple conflicting stories—what folklorists call *variants*, evidence of the transmission process that produces folklore (Brunvand 1978, 7). Dissemination of the tales prompts more sightings from imaginative individuals, giving the supposed ghosts something of a life of their own.

Other Phenomena

In addition to visual apparitions, other touted phenomena at lighthouses (and their environs) are similar to those reported at other alleged spirit-dwelling sites. They include the following:

Ghostly footsteps. The sounds of footfalls are frequently reported in haunted lighthouses or keepers' homes. This is despite the irony of ghosts being such ethereal entities that they pass through walls yet allegedly depressing floorboards as they walk.

My wife Diana and I failed to hear the footsteps that have been reported in the lightkeeper's dwelling at Seul Choix (pronounced Sis-shwa) on Lake Michigan (again, see Figure 1). Supposedly, they were heard once by a carpenter while he was nailing subflooring at the base of the staircase. Because the footsteps stopped whenever he ceased nailing, he concluded that the sounds were merely echoes of his hammering—that is, until he finally put down his hammer and still heard "heavy footsteps" upstairs. Reportedly he "packed up his tools and left, 'vowing never to return by himself'" (Elizabeth and Roberts 1999, 85–86).

The precise truth of this tale is anybody's guess, but there are a number of likely causes for audible footstep-like noises in a "haunted" place. Among them are simple creaking sounds caused by an old building's settling, from woodwork that yields knocking and popping sounds as the result of temperature changes, or from myriad other causes (Nickell 1995, 47–48; Christopher 1970, 169, 171). At Thirty Mile Point Light on Lake Ontario, one overnight guest commented in the log book, "People write of ghosts. We haven't heard any yet, just a lot of noises from the pipes when the heat turns on!" (Thirty 2001–2007).

Still another force seems a likely culprit for the "footsteps" heard in the tower of Battery Point Lighthouse near Crescent City, California. They invariably occurred "during stormy weather," indicating that the sounds were probably caused by the wind. Although previous keepers had experienced many such "ghostly" happenings at Battery Point, a subsequent couple did not. The wife attributed her lack of haunting incidents to the fact that she absolutely did not believe in ghosts (Elizabeth and Roberts 1999, 50–63).

Moans and shrieks. Eerie sounds attributed to mournful or distraught spirits are commonly reported—as if vocalizations are possible without a larynx. In one instance, such sounds were found to come from the wind blowing through an open sewer pipe. Comments William O. Thompson in his *Lighthouse Legends and Hauntings* (1998, 33), "Perhaps this is how some of our ghost stories get started. Every lighthouse is exposed to strange sounds and an active imagination can be very creative."

Consider New Presque Isle Light Station on Lake Huron (north of Alpena, Michigan). According to ghost mongers, the site is haunted by the unrequited spirit of a former keeper's wife. She went insane (according to one version of the tale) due to the stark isolation and numbing boredom of lighthouse life or (says another version) due to being locked in the tower whenever her husband visited his mistress in town. In any event, the woman supposedly died at the site, and "people have reported hearing her screaming" near the tower. In a rare moment of skepticism, however, the writers concede, "perhaps it's just the fierce Lake Huron wind screaming around the tower" (Elizabeth and Roberts 1999, 12).

Thompson (1998, 73) observes that lighthouses are "natural places" for people to have "ghostly experiences," and he mentions the effects of wind whistling through cracks in the structures as among the causes of unaccountable noises. As well, analogous to what happens to woodwork, he notes, old steel "creeps and moans" due to expansion by sunlight and contraction by cold night air.

Again, at Thirty Mile Point Light, guest-book entries report various ghostly sounds, while others give skeptical interpretations, like this one: "Ghosts? Well we heard all kinds of strange noises but it was very windy." Another person wrote, "The very windy nights added to the 'ghostly sounds' of the building" (Thirty 2001–2007).

Phantom smells. Among other "ghostly" phenomena at lighthouses are strange smells. For example, from Old Presque Isle Lighthouse, now a museum, comes a touching story by Lorraine Parris, a worker in the gift shop. Previously, she and her husband George were caretakers at the site for four-teen years, until he died of a heart attack at the beginning of 1992. According to *Lighthouse Ghosts* (Elizabeth and Roberts 1999, 8), "Sometimes she feels George in the dwelling with her." Moreover, "She recalls waking up some mornings smelling eggs and sausage cooking—a familiar aroma since that's what George used to cook for her for breakfast every morning." But surely, rather than a ghostly visitation the experience is instead the poignant effect of a memory arising lovingly from the subconscious.

At other sites, such as St. Augustine Lighthouse, the motif of lingering cigar smoke appears in circulating ghost tales (Elizabeth and Roberts 1999, 40–49). Again, combined with the previously mentioned footsteps in the keeper's house at Seul Choix Point Lighthouse, the "strong smell of cigars" convinces some "that a lighthouse keeper is still at work" there ("Seul Choix" 2005), although others attribute the phenomena to a ship's captain named James Townshend who died in the dwelling in 1910 (Elizabeth and Roberts 1999, 82–89; Smith 2003, 124).

However, not only is the identity of the phantom questioned but so is the nature of the smoke itself. In her *Ghost Stories of the Sea*, Barbara Smith (2003, 124) attributes the phenomenon to Captain Townshend but refers to it as "the smell of the man's ever-present *cigarettes*," again stating that "the smoky smell from the man's *cigarettes* can still occasionally be detected" (emphasis added). Here, I think, is an impor-tant clue to what is really happening. The smell of actual smoke—whether from area chimneys or cigarettes or whatever other source—is interpreted as cigar smoke because that is what has been suggested and is therefore expected.

Proof of this is evident from an incident at Seul Choix reported in *Haunted Lakes II* (Stonehouse 2000, 4). Two visitors, smelling what they thought was burning wiring, ran to tell the tour guide they thought the house was on fire. If "cigar smoke" can be mistaken for burning wiring, some other burning material could in turn be mistaken for it.

Pranks. Mischief attributed to ghosts at various sites may have a far simpler explanation: the pranksters may not be dead after all!

Consider, for instance, the shenanigans attributed to the aforementioned spectral cigar smoker at Seul Choix. Supposedly the ghost of Captain Townshend liked to "play pranks." A docent claims that

> . . . he sometimes turns over the silverware on the table (Captain Townshend used to hold his fork upside down when he ate). Once in a while the old captain shuts the Bible that's on display in the dwelling, and he seems to take great pleasure in turning the hat around on the mannequin that's dressed in an official keeper's uniform. Occasionally, Captain Townshend even puts a cigar or two in the pocket of the keeper's coat! (Elizabeth and Roberts 1999, 87)

No, the cigars were not materialized from the Great Beyond. They had been set out "in strategic places in the house," once by a group doing a magazine story and again by a couple of Boy Scouts and their Scoutmaster (Stonehouse 2000, 10). The temptation each time for someone to play ghost must have been irresistible. Over the years I have encountered many such pranksters (Nickell 2001), even catching a few red-handed myself (Nickell 2008).

Phantom Light

The Old Presque Isle Light, first lit in 1840, was extinguished when the "New" lighthouse was built about a mile away in 1870. Yet according to some, the spirit of an old keeper still maintains a "phantom light" in the tower, which has been witnessed on numerous occasions.

Nevertheless, there are reasons to believe that whatever is the source of the mystery light, it has nothing to do with spirits. It is crucial to note that it is never seen by anyone who is actually inside the lantern room. And it is described as lacking the intensity and whiteness of a true lighthouse beam. Indeed, it is not a beam at all (see the photo in Grant and Jones 2002, 139), and certainly not a rotating beam, but tends to be only a "yellow glow" (Elizabeth and Roberts 1999, 6).

Indeed, I think we can take a clue from similar reports; the motif of a ghost light is common in spooklore. The late magician and psychic investigator Milbourne Christopher (1970, 172–173) told of a deserted house wherein persons at a distance from the structure could see a lantern, supposedly carried by a specter, moving from room to room. It always went from right to left. However, an investigator discovered that the light was not an interior one at all but rather the reflection of headlights on the window's glass each time a car approached the house. Other spirit lights in windows often turn out to be reflections from the moon or other light sources, an effect I have witnessed on more than one occasion (Nickell 1995, 50–51).

Now, we are told that attempts have been made to stop Presque Isle's phantom light from shining. "We've had the glass covered inside and the lens covered, but the light was still there," says Lorraine Parris. "It seems to shine right through. There's just no way to stop it" (qtd. in Grant and Jones 2002, 139). Reportedly, coast guardsmen remained baffled as the light persisted even when nearby lights were extinguished for a while one night (Elizabeth and Roberts 199, 6).

But all such actions are obviously predicated on the assumption that reflection is the logical culprit. Indeed the fact that the light still shone after the glass was covered on the *inside* is telling: it seems a safe bet that it would not continue if the glass were covered on the *outside*. Moreover, the reflection hypothesis is given weight by the light's dependence on viewing conditions. It is reportedly best seen from a certain spot on the pier. Also, if the viewer is traveling along the road near the marina or in a boat on the lake, the "spirit light" will "blink on and off," thus "making it appear to be the beam from a rotating beacon"—while it is, of course, no such thing. That effect may well be due to a light reflecting first from one flat pane of glass then another as the viewer's line of sight changes. And so it appears that here, as with other lighthouses, ghosts are really only illusions of our sometimes haunted minds.

Acknowledgments

Thanks to Pat Beauchamp and CFI Libraries Director Tim Binga for their assistance with this article.

References

Brunvand, Jan Harold. 1978. *The Study of American Folklore: An Introduction*, 2nd ed. New York: W.W. Norton.

Christopher, Milbourne. 1970. *ESP, Seers and Psychics*. New York: Thomas Y. Crowell Co.

Elizabeth, Norma, and Bruce Roberts. 1999. *Lighthouse Ghosts: 13 Bona Fide Apparitions Standing Watch Over America's Shores*. N.p. Crane Hill Publishers.

———. 2004. *Lighthouse Ghosts and Carolina Coastal Legends*. Morehead City, N.C.: Lighthouse Publications.

Grant, John, and Ray Jones. 2002. *Legendary Lighthouses*, vol. II. Guilford, Conn.: Globe Pequot Press.

Guiley, Rosemary Ellen. 2000. *The Encyclopedia of Ghosts and Spirits*. New York: Checkmark Books.

Hermanson, Don. N.d. *True Lighthouse Hauntings* (video).

Nickell, Joe. 1995. *Entities: Angels, Spirits, Demons, and Other Alien Beings*. Amherst, N.Y.: Prometheus Books.

————. 2001. Phantoms, frauds, or fantasies? In James Houran and Rense Lange *Hauntings and Poltergeists: Multidisciplinary Perspectives.* Jefferson, N.C.: McFarland and Co., 214–223.

————. 2008. Catching ghosts. *Skeptical Briefs,* 18:2 (June), 4–6.

"Peggy's Cove, Lady In Blue." 2008a. Creepy Canada, Season 2—Episode 3. Available online at www.creepy.tv/season2_e3.html; accessed February 18, 2008.

"Peggy's Cove, Nova Scotia, Lady In Blue." 2008b. Ghost Study message board. Available online at www.paranormalsoup.com/forums/index.php?showtopic=21962&mode=threaded; accessed February 18, 2008.

Seul Choix Point Lighthouse. 2005. Available online at www.exploringthenorth.com/seulchoix/seul.html; accessed October 4, 2005.

Smith, Barbara. 2003. *Ghost Stories of the Sea.* Edmonton, Alberta: Ghost House Books.

Stonehouse, Frederick. 1997. *Haunted Lakes: Great Lakes Ghost Stories, Superstitions and Sea Serpents.* Duluth, Minnesota: Lake Superior Port Cities.

————. 2000. *Haunted Lakes II: More Great Ghost Stories.* Duluth Minnesota: Lake Superior Port Cities.

Thirty Mile Point Light. 2001–2007. Guest books 1–3, various entries; copies in author's files.

Thompson, William O. 1998. *Lighthouse Legends and Hauntings.* Kennebunk, Maine: 'Scapes Me.

Tyrrell, G.N.M. 1973. *Apparitions.* London: The Society for Psychical Research (org. publ. 1943, rev. 1953).

Zepke, Terrance. 1999. *Ghosts of the Carolina Coasts: Haunted Lighthouses, Plantations, and Other Historic Sites.* Sarasota, Florida: Pineapple Press.

A Skeleton's Tale

More than half a century after modern spiritualism began with purported communications from the ghost of a murdered peddler, the reality of the messages was allegedly confirmed. A skeleton was reportedly uncovered in the cellar of the original farmhouse where the séances had taken place along with the peddler's tin trunk. Now, a century after that, the claims are again being touted by spiritualists who have enshrined the excavated foundation (Figure 1)—sort of a spiritualists' equivalent of the Mormons' Hill Cumorah (where Joseph Smith claimed he received a book written on gold plates from the angel Moroni [Nickell 2004]). Assisted by research librarian Timothy Binga, director of Center for Inquiry Libraries, I sought to uncover the true facts in the case.

Background

Modern spiritualism began in Hydesville, New York, in 1848. At the home of a blacksmith named John Fox, strange rapping noises began to occur in the bedroom of Fox's young daughters, Margaret ("Maggie") and Katharine ("Katie"). The girls claimed the noises were communications from the departed spirit of a murdered peddler. After a time, on the night of March 31 (All Fool's Eve!), the girls' mother witnessed a remarkable demonstration that she later described in a signed report.

Loudly, Katie addressed "Mr. Splitfoot," saying, "do as I do," and clapping her hands. At once, there came the same number of mysterious raps. Next Maggie exclaimed, "Now do just as I do; count one, two, three, four," clapping her hands accordingly. Four raps came in response (Mulholland 1938, 30–33).

Figure 1. CFI Libraries Director Tim Binga stands at the enshrined site of the birthplace of Spiritualism. (Photo by Joe Nickell)

Next, the peddler's spirit began to answer questions by rapping, once for no, twice for yes. He claimed he had been murdered and his body buried in the cellar, but digging there produced only a few bones attributed to animals (Weisberg 2004, 57).

Before long, people discovered that the girls could conjure up not only the ghostly peddler but other obliging spirits as well. The demonstrations received such attention that the girls' older sister, Leah Fish, originated a "spiritualistic" society. "Spiritualism" began to take on the trappings of religion, with hymns being sung at the opening and close of a session (which they called a "séance"). Following a successful visit to New York, Leah took the girls on tour to towns and cities across the nation. Everywhere people were anxious to communicate with the souls of their departed loved ones.

However, scientists and other rational-minded investigators came forth to challenge Maggie and Katie's claims. Early on, University of Buffalo faculty members studied the girls' raps. The examiners excluded "spiritual causation" and asserted, curiously enough, that the raps were "produced by the action of the will, through voluntary action on the joints." In a much later investigation, the "spirits" gave out erroneous information, and investigators caused the rapping sounds to cease abruptly by controlling Margaret's feet (Mulholland 1938, 34–38).

Then, four decades after spiritualism began, sisters Margaret Fox Kane and Katherine Fox Jencken confessed it had all been a trick. On Sunday, October 21, 1888, the sisters appeared at the Academy of Music in New York City. With Katherine sitting in a box and repeatedly nodding in agreement while a number of spiritualists expressed their disapproval with groans and hisses, Margaret revealed all from the music hall stage. She explained how she had produced the rapping noises by slipping her foot from her shoe and snapping her toes. Placing her stockinged foot on a thin plank, she demonstrated the effect for the audience. As *The Evening Post* reported the following day, "Mrs. Kane now locates the origin of Modern Spiritualism in her great toe" (qtd. in Christopher 1970, 181). Margaret went on to state:

> I think that it is about time that the truth of this miserable subject "Spiritualism" should be brought out. It is now widespread all over the world, and unless it is put down it will do great evil. I was the first in the field and I have the right to expose it.
>
> My sister Katie and myself were very young children when this horrible deception began. I was eight and just a year and a half older than she. We were very mischievous children and we wanted to terrify our dear mother, who was a very good woman and very easily frightened. At night when we were in bed, we used to tie an apple to a string and move it up and down, causing the apple to bump on the floor, or we would drop the apple on the floor, making a strange noise every time it would rebound. Mother listened to this for a time. She could not understand it and did not suspect us of being capable of a trick because we were so young.
>
> At last she could stand it no longer and she called the neighbors in and told them about it. It was this that set us to discover the means of making the raps.

Margaret explained:

> My sister Katie was the first one to discover that by swishing her fingers she could produce a certain noise with the knuckles and joints, and that the same effect could be made with the toes. Finding we could make raps with our feet—first with one foot and then with both—we practiced until we could do this easily when the room was dark. (qtd. in Mulholland 1938, 41–42)

Margaret also stated that Leah knew the spirit rappings were fake, and that when she traveled with the girls (on their first nationwide tour) it was she who signaled the answers to various questions. (She probably chatted with sitters before the séance to obtain information; when that did not produce the requisite facts, the "spirits" no doubt spoke in vague generalizations that are the mainstay of spiritualistic charlatans.)

Margaret repeated her exposé in other cities close to New York. However, explains John Mulholland (1938, 43), "It was expected that this would give her sufficient income to live but she shortly discovered that while many people will pay to be humbugged few will pay to be educated."

Perhaps not surprisingly, then, Margaret returned to mediumship when she needed money again. After her death on March 8, 1895, thousands of spiritualist mourners attended her funeral.

Today, spiritualists characterize Margaret's exposé as bogus, attributing it to her need for money or the desire for revenge against her rivals or both. However, not only were her admissions fully corroborated by her sister, but she demonstrated to the audience that she could produce the mysterious raps just as she said (Christopher 1970, 181).

The Discovery

The Fox sisters had seemingly fooled the world, but after the turn of the century, new evidence for their supposed genuineness was allegedly discovered. As reported by the *Boston Journal* of November 23, 1904:

> The skeleton of the man who first caused the rappings heard by the Fox Sisters in 1848 has been found between the walls of the house occupied by the sisters, and clears them from the only shadow of doubt held concerning their sincerity in the discovery of spirit communication.
>
> The Fox sisters declared that they learned to communicate with the spirit of a man, and that he told them he had been murdered and buried in the cellar. Evacuation failed to locate the body and thus give proof positive of their story.

The *Journal* continued:

> The discovery was made by school children playing in the cellar of the building in Hydesville known as "The Spook House," where the Fox sisters first heard the wonderful rappings. A reputable citizen of Clyde, who owns the house, made an investigation, and found an almost entire human skeleton between the crumbling walls, undoubtedly that of the wandering peddler who it was claimed was murdered in the east room and buried in the basement.
>
> Examination revealed that a false and unobserved inner wall had been built. Between this false inner wall and the original outer wall and near the center of the basement, the skeleton was found. It is interesting to know that the false wall is composed of stones like those used fifty years ago to build stone fences. This recalls a statement made over

fifty years ago by Miss Lucretia Pulver, that Mr. Bell [the earlier house owner and presumed murderer] worked each night under cover of darkness, carrying stones from the fence into the cellar. The finding of the bones corroborates the sworn statement made by Margaret Fox [the girls' mother], April 11, 1848. . . . (qtd. in Muldoon 1942, 20–24)

Additional stories appeared in other newspapers ("Bones" 1904; "Fox" 1904; "Headless" 1904; "Topics" 1904).

This reputed discovery was trumpeted by spiritualists over the following decades, along with a "tin peddler's pack"—actually a tin trunk (Figure 2)—that was allegedly discovered at the same site (Keeler 1922, 60). The trunk was later kept in the cottage that had been moved to Lily Dale spiritualist village in 1916 and used as a museum. The cottage

Figure 2. Joe Nickell examines the alleged "peddler's trunk" at Lily Dale Museum. (Photo by Diana Harris)

remained there until it was destroyed by fire in the 1950s. While the trunk was saved, skeptics have long questioned its authenticity (Weisberg 2004, 266–267).

Investigation

To review the alleged discoveries at the Fox cottage's cellar, I twice visited the site, taking photographs and making a diagrammatic sketch of the stone structure; interviewed knowledgeable persons; examined Fox-related artifacts, including the reputed peddler's trunk at the Lily Dale spiritualist museum; with Tim Binga, conducted research at the Public Library at Newark, N.Y. (where I joked that my work was so important I had "brought my own librarian"); and studied a valuable collection of old papers, clippings, and photographs that were generously sent over to the library for our use by the Newark-Arcadia Historical Society. We also sought out rare books and journals and did much other work, all of it demanding but ultimately paying dividends.

Unfortunately, as it happens, there is reason for skepticism of nearly every aspect of the case. To begin with, the earliest published testimonies never gave the peddler's name, only the initials "C.B.," with the B specifically applying to the surname (Lewis 1848, 10). Only later was the name said to be "Charles B. Rosna" or some variant; Sir Arthur Conan Doyle (1926, I: 64, 76) insisted it was actually "Charles B. Rosma." Another source gives "Charles Rosa" (Guiley 2000, 141).

In fact, no one has been able to find a single record or other proof of the existence of a peddler named Charles B. Rosna/Rosma/Rosa. One source (Pressing N.d., 63) was forced to conclude, lamely, that the name "might have been misspelled," but no peddler with any similar name has ever been identified. We too looked—in vain.

At the old cottage site we studied the restored foundation and its double wall, the "false" interior one having ostensibly been placed secretly to hide the peddler's corpse (Muldoon 1942, 20–21; Keeler 1922). However, it is apparent that the wall in question is actually just one of four inner walls that likely represent an original, boxlike foundation (Figure 3). That foundation was apparently later enlarged into a rectangular shape by the addition of new walls around the old ones (creating unequal spaces between the walls at either end and thickening the front and rear walls at the same time). Perhaps the extra foundation resulted from the house having been expanded from a cabin into a cottage. We later discovered that the "two separate stone foundations" were confirmed in 1904 ("Headless" 1904).

As to the bones themselves, their authenticity was questioned at the time of their alleged discovery. The *New York Times* ("Topics" 1904) reported that the bones had created a stir "amusingly disproportioned to any necessary significance of the discovery." That was because there was no proof either that the bones belonged to the "legendary peddler" or that the Fox sisters had done anything more than capitalize on a then-current rumor that a peddler was murdered at the site. The *Times* said of spiritualists' claims about the bones, "As usual, they are taking all pos-

Figure 3. A reputedly false inner wall (left) of Fox cottage is actually only part of a smaller, four-walled, inner foundation. (Photo by Joe Nickell)

sible pains to render a real investigation of the affair impossible, and are assuming as true a lot of things much in need of other proof than their own assertions."

The Acadian Weekly ("Fox" 1904) opined that while the bones might have been hidden in the wall for half a century, they might equally have been "disinterred from some cemetery and placed there for effect." The paper referred to the original 1848 story of spirit communication at the cottage as "the old hoax."

Eventually, the true source of the bones was reported in an editorial in the *Journal of the American Society for Psychical Research* in 1909. A physician had been asked by another publication (the *Occult Review*) to investigate the alleged discovery:

> He reports to us that he found a number of bones there, but that there were only a few ribs with odds and ends of bones and among them a superabundance of some and a deficiency of others. Among them also were some chicken bones. There was nothing about the premises to indicate that they had been buried there, but might have been put there by boys in sport. He also reports that within a few days past he has learned that a certain person near the place had put the bones there as a practical joke and is now too much ashamed of it to confess it. Whether there is any better foundation for these incidents than for the original story it is not possible to decide, but it is certain that the probabilities that there is anything more than a casual coincidence or than a trick played on the credulity of the defenders of the Fox sisters are very much shaded. (Editorial 1909)

But then what about the peddler's trunk, allegedly found at the same site and time as the bones? As a matter of fact, the trunk was never reported in any of the contemporary sources we uncovered. The earliest mention of it I have found is an account penned years later by one P.L.O.A. Keeler (1922), a Lily Dale medium who had a reputation for faking spirit writing and other phenomena (Nickell 2007). I examined the trunk at the Lily Dale museum, whose curator Ron Nagy (2006) conceded there was no real provenance for it nor any proof of its discovery in 1904. And the trunk's condition appears far too good for its supposed half-century burial (Figure 2).

Conclusions

The modern unearthing of the Fox cottage's foundations did nothing to support the claim that in 1848 schoolgirls had communicated with the spirit of a murdered peddler. Instead, the excavation made it possible for everyone to see that no "false wall" had been built to hide the legendary peddler's remains but that it was merely part of an earlier, smaller foundation. The best evidence indicates that the 1904 "discovery" of the peddler's bones was a hoax; ditto the later appearance of the tin trunk. Therefore, the Fox sisters' confessions stand, corroborated by independent evidence that the spirit rappings they produced were accomplished by trickery.

Acknowledgments

In addition to Tim Binga, I was assisted by many others, including my wife, Diana Harris, and Paul E. Loynes who did the typesetting. I also wish to thank the helpful staff of the Newark Public Library and the Newark-Arcadia Historical Society (notably John Zornow and Chris Davis), Ron Nagy at Lily Dale, and Judge Harold Stiles.

References

Bones in 'old spook house.' 1904. New York Times, November 23.
Cadwallader, M.E. 1922. Hydesville in History. Chicago: Progressive Thinker.
Christopher, Milbourne. 1970. ESP, Seers and Psychics. New York: Thomas Y. Crowell.
Conan Doyle, Arthur. 1926. The History of Spiritualism, in two vols. Reprinted New York: Arno Press, 1975.
Editorial. 1909. Journal of the American Society for Psychical Research. March, 191.
The Fox House figures again in a sensation. 1904. The Arcadian Weekly Gazette, November 23.
Guiley, Rosemary Ellen. 2000. The Encyclopedia of Ghosts and Spirits. New York: Checkmark Books.
Headless skeleton in Fox Sisters' home. 1904. New York Times, November 24.
Keeler, P.L.O.A. 1922. The skeleton in the Fox cottage, in Cadwallader 1922, 59–60.
Lewis, E.E. 1848. A Report of the Mysterious Noises Heard in the House of Mr. John D. Fox, in Hydesville, Arcadia, Wayne County [N.Y.]. Canandaigua, N.Y.: E.E. Lewis.
Muldoon, Sylvan. 1942. Famous Psychic Stories, Psychic Series Volume II. Darlington, Wisconsin: The New Horizon Publishers.
Mulholland, John. 1938. Beware Familiar Spirits. Reprinted New York: Charles Scribner's Sons, 1979.
Nagy, Ron. 2006. Interview by Joe Nickell and Diana Harris, September 1.
Nickell, Joe. 2004. Joseph Smith: A matter of visions. Chap. 35 of The Mystery Chronicles. Lexington, Ky.: The University Press of Kentucky, 296–303.
———. 2007. Adventures in Paranormal Investigation. Lexington, Ky.: The University Press of Kentucky.
Pressing, R.G. N.d. Rappings That Startled the World. Lily Dale, N.Y.: Dale News.
Topics of the Times. 1904. New York Times, November 25.
Weisberg, Barbara. 2004. Talking to the Dead. New York: HarperSanFrancisco.

Return to Roswell

Conspiracy theorists notwithstanding, the crash of a supposed flying saucer near Roswell, New Mexico, in mid-1947 has been effectively explained as something much more mundane: a balloon-borne device. Yet Roswell zealots continue to try to debunk the debunking. New claims—that the Roswell "debris field" described by eyewitnesses was too extensive to have resulted from a crashed balloon array—are being touted. The research was tested experimentally in the Discovery Channel documentary, *Best Evidence: The Roswell Incident* (2007). I was asked to observe and comment on the experiment, and here is my own report on the matter for *Skeptical Inquirer* readers.

Background

On July 8, 1947, an unauthorized press release from an eager but relatively inexperienced public information officer at New Mexico's Roswell Army Air Field propelled the "Roswell Incident" into history. He reported that a "flying disc" had been recovered from an area ranch where it had crashed (Berlitz and Moore 1980; Korff 1997). The crash came in the wake of the first modern UFO sighting, witnessed by private pilot Kenneth Arnold on June 24. Arnold's string of "flying saucers" may well have been nothing more than mirage effects caused by a temperature inversion (McGaha 2006), but it initiated the modern wave of UFO sightings (Nickell 2007).

Soon after the Roswell press release made worldwide newspaper headlines, the young officer was reprimanded and new information was announced: the unidentified flying object had really been a weather balloon, said officials. Photographs of the wreckage matched descriptions of the debris given by the rancher W.W. "Mac" Brazel, who discovered it on his rented property, the Foster ranch. In the *Roswell Daily Record* (July 9, 1947), Brazel described (in a reporter's words) "a large area of bright wreckage" consisting of tinfoil, rubber strips, tough paper, sticks, and tape with flower designs. "There was no sign of any metal in the area," noted the newspaper story, "which might have been used for an engine and no sign of any propellers of any kind"("Harassed rancher" 1947).

Although officials announced that the UFO had simply been a weather balloon, the best evidence now indicates that the crashed device was really a United States government spy balloon—actually a balloon-array with dangling radar reflectors. Part of Project Mogul, it was used in an attempt to monitor sonic emissions from anticipated nuclear tests by the Soviet Union. I spoke about this with former Project Mogul scientist Charles B. Moore, who identified the Roswell wreckage in photographs as likely coming from a lost Flight 4 Mogul array. (See, importantly, Dave Thomas's special report in the July/August 1995 *Skeptical Inquirer*. See also *The Roswell Report: Case Closed* published by the United States Air Force [U.S. Air Force 1997].)

Continuing Saga

The news story died almost immediately, but the event continued as the subject of folklore and fakelore. In addition to the dubious "memories" of aging Roswellians, there emerged amateurishly forged government-conspiracy documents[1] and a hoaxed "alien autopsy" film showing the purported dissection of one of the extraterrestrials allegedly recovered from the crash site (Nickell 2001, 118–121). Many have given free rein to their imaginations (see Figure 1).

Enter Robert Galganski. A crash-safety research engineer and a Roswell buff, he offered a paper, "The Roswell Debris Field: An Engineer's Perspective" (published by Fund for UFO Research). In it, Galganski (2005, vii) used "existing documentation" in order "to calculate a very liberal quantity—that is, significantly more than one would expect—of debris that [Mogul] Flight 4 could have deposited on the ranch pasture."

Essentially, Galganski examined the Roswell controversy *quantitatively*, focusing on the *amount* of the debris. As he summed up, "These quantitative and visual findings provide compelling support for the conclusion, based on logic and common sense, which many other researchers have reached: Project Mogul Flight 4 did *not* cause the Roswell debris field" (Galganski 2005, vii).

Figure 1. The "Roswell Incident" has been transformed from a mundane occurrence into a sensational science fantasy, as in this mural in the Roswell UFO Museum. (Photo by Joe Nickell)

The Test

Galganski based his findings on two main sources. One was Major Jesse Marcel, who in 1947 was the Roswell Army Air Field staff intelligence officer. The other was Mac Brazel, the rancher who discovered the crash site. As Galganski concedes, however, the two descriptions were "markedly different" (2005, vii).

Indeed, Marcel—recalling more than thirty-two years later—stated that the field was ". . . three-quarters of a mile long and two hundred to three hundred feet wide," whereas Mac Brazel described the debris as only (in the reporter's words) "scattered over an area about 200 yards in diameter" ("Harassed rancher" 1947).[2] After making numerous assumptions and performing myriad calculations, Galganski determined that the field would have been covered by the wreckage so sparsely that it could not "honestly be called a 'debris field'" (2005, 28).

To test his conclusions, the production company for the Discovery Channel documentary recreated a Mogul-type array, crashed it, and assessed the resulting amount of debris. They chose a site in California at the edge of the Mojave Airport, and I was asked to monitor the experiment. (The experiment took place the next day, December 20, 2006, and the documentary aired February 22, 2007.)

The crew, including a Hollywood special effects technician, recreated *one-half* of a Mogul array. For this, they inflated a dozen four-foot balloons, attaching one after the other to a tethered line, then strung on three box-kite-like replica radar reflectors (consisting of sticks and foil-covered paper—Figure 2), and finally attached a parachute carrying a simulated radiosonde (instrument package). Then a rifleman used an air-gun to burst each balloon in turn until the wreckage lay scattered on the ground. Galganski thought the debris was insufficient to match that at

Figure 2. A replica of one-half of a Project Mogul spy balloon array was created for the Discovery Channel. (Photo by Joe Nickell)

Figure 3. Shot down, the device, having been tethered, left debris less broken up and scattered than otherwise would have been expected. (Photo by Joe Nickell)

Roswell in 1947, but since the array had been kept on a tether, the debris naturally came down and littered a very limited area, only about 79 × 138 feet (Figure 3). Had it been more broken up and scattered by the wind, I concluded, the results would have been dramatically different.

Wrong Assumptions

We must recognize that Galganski is at pains to assume that a large wreckage area and a consequent amount of debris was needed to at least "lightly litter" the area. From this perspective, he believes that what crashed at Roswell was much, much larger than a Flight 4 Mogul balloon train. This seems a very poor way to make a determination. One wonders what Galganski would conclude from the size of the area strewn by debris from the U.S. Space Shuttle Columbia disaster (on February 1, 2003). Officials said, according to *The New York Times*, that "The grim fallout scattered along a path at least 100 miles long and 10 miles wide," (Halbfinger and Oppel 2003). Was a gigantic space shuttle involved?

In fact, it is Galganski (2005, 45) who assumes "a litter-filled region," not Mac Brazel. Brazel provided not only an estimate of the size of the area involved but also indicated the amount of debris. Brazel, Major Marcel, and a couple of others took the pieces to Brazel's home (a now-deserted house I visited with investigator Vaughn Rees in 2003—see Figure 4). *The Roswell Daily Record* reported:

> According to Brazel they simply could not reconstruct it at all. They tried to make a kite out of it, but could not do that and could not find any

Figure 4. The author at the now-deserted old farmhouse on the Foster ranch where Mac Brazel lived when he discovered the infamous Roswell wreckage. (Author's photo by Vaughn Rees)

way to put it back together so that it would fit.

Then Major Marcel brought it to Roswell, and that was the last he heard of it until the story broke that he had found a flying disc.

The newspaper article continued:

Brazel said that he did not see it fall from the sky and did not see it before it was torn, so he did not know the size or shape it might have been, but he thought it might have been about as large as a table top. The balloon which held it up, if that was how it worked, must have been about 12 feet long, he felt, measuring the distance by the size of the room in which he sat. The rubber was smoky gray in color and scattered over an area about 200 yards in diameter.

The article went on to add:

When the debris was gathered up the tinfoil, paper, tape, and sticks made a bundle about three feet long and 7 or 8 inches thick, while the rubber made a bundle about 18 or 20 inches long and about 8 inches thick. In all, he estimated, the entire lot would have weighed maybe five pounds.

A small and lightweight "disc" indeed! Clearly, what Brazel described was not even an entire Mogul array. The article added that "No strings or wire were to be found but there were some eyelets in the paper to indicate that some sort of attachment may have been used" ("Harassed rancher" 1947).

Photographs made of the wreckage when it was displayed to the news media (U.S. Air Force 1997, 7) show that the wreckage was consistent with Brazel's description and that it in turn matches Project Mogul's Flight 4 balloon/radar-reflector array.

From the evidence, we see that not only did balloons burst near Roswell in 1947 but that conspiracy theorists have had their fanciful flying-saucer bubbles burst as well.

Acknowledgments

Thanks to Vaughn Rees and Tim Binga for their assistance with this and earlier Roswell research, as well as the entire crew I worked with in the Mojave Desert, assembled by Creative Differences Productions, Toronto.

Notes

1. These "MJ-12 documents" fooled arch Roswell-conspiracy writer Stanton T. Friedman, who has continued to tout the bogus documents (Friedman 1996). See Nickell and Fischer 1990.

2. Among other sources were two that gave estimates ranging from only "about 20 feet square" (a Capt. Sheridan Cavitt, whose testimony Galganski finds dubious) to debris being "scattered over a square mile" (given in an Associated Press article). See Galganski 2005, 24–25.

References

Berlitz, Charles, and William L. Moore. 1980. *The Roswell Incident*. New York: Grosset & Dunlap.

Best Evidence: The Roswell Incident. 2007. Television documentary on Discovery Channel, February 22.

Friedman, Stanton T. 1996. *Top Secret/Magic*. New York: Marlowe & Company.

Galganski, Robert. 2005. *The Roswell Debris Field: An Engineer's Perspective*; third ed. Washington, D.C.: Fund for UFO Research.

Halbfinger, David M., and Richard A. Oppel Jr. 2003. Loss of the shuttle: On the ground. *The New York Times* (February 2).

Harassed rancher who located 'saucer' sorry he told about it. 1947. *The Roswell Daily Record*, July 9; copy given in Galganski 2005, C-1.

Korff, Kal K. 1997. What really happened at Roswell? *Skeptical Inquirer* 21(4) (July/August): 24–30.

McGaha, James. 2006. Interview by Joe Nickell, September 28–29; in Nickell 2007, 14–16.

Nickell, Joe, and John F. Fischer. 1990. The crashed-saucer forgeries. *International UFO Reporter* (March/April).

———. 2001. *Real-Life X-Files: Investigating the Paranormal*. Lexington, Ky.: University Press of Kentucky.

———. 2007. Mysterious entities of the Pacific Northwest, part II. *Skeptical Inquirer* 31(2) (March/April): 14–17.

Thomas, Dave. 1995. The Roswell incident and Project Mogul: Scientist participant supports direct links. *Skeptical Inquirer* 19(4) (July/August): 15–18.

U.S. Air Force. The Roswell Report: Case Closed. 1997. Authored by Captain James McAndrew for Headquarters USAF; Washington, D.C.: U.S. Government Printing Office.

Eucharistic 'Miracles'

Did an incident that reportedly occurred in Turin, Italy, in 1453 (unrelated to the famous "shroud" later enshrined there[1]) offer unimpeachable evidence of the supernatural? How else can one explain the wonderful story of "The Miracle of Turin" and other Eucharistic miracle claims?

Introduction

In her book *Eucharistic Miracles*, Joan Carroll Cruz (1987, xi) states, "The greatest treasure in the Catholic Church is, without question, the Holy Eucharist—in which Jesus Christ humbly assumes the appearance of bread." In Catholicism, the Eucharist is the sacrament in which the bread and wine consumed at Communion in remembrance of Jesus's Last Supper are, by the miracle of "transubstantiation," changed into the actual body and blood of Christ, whence they are known as the Blessed Sacrament (Stravinskas 2002, 139, 302, 734). In other words, Catholics take literally Jesus's statement regarding the bread: "Take, eat: this is my body," and regarding the wine, "Drink ye all of it; for this is my blood of the new testament, which is shed for many for the remission of sins" (Matt. 26: 26–28).

In contrast, Protestants understand the story (given in various other versions: Mark 14: 22–25; Luke 22: 19, 20[2]; John 6: 48–58; and 1 Cor. 11: 23–26) as symbolic of Jesus's dying for mankind. Indeed, it is an evolved form of the Jewish Passover ritual (Dummelow 1951, 710). Religious writers Marcus J. Borg and John Dominic Crossan (2006, 192–194) consider the story, together with the entire Easter narrative, as a parable (a simple story with a moral, whether factually true or not).

Eucharistic Miracles

Nevertheless, Transubstantiation is a dogma of Catholicism and, from at least the eighth century, numerous "Eucharistic miracles" that seem to verify its reality have been reported. In addition to a few dozen accounts in Cruz (1987), many more are related in *Legends of the Blessed Sacrament* (Shapcote 1877), and no fewer than 142 are featured in a Vatican international traveling exhibition titled the "Eucharistic Miracles of the World," which I was able to view in Lackawanna, New York, on September 20, 2007. (The exhibition consists of display panels, otherwise available on a website [Eucharist 2007].)

Some Eucharistic miracle tales (Cruz 1987, 187–188, 191–192, 208–209) seem to be little more than derivations of biblical stories. For example, the account of a boy having eaten communion bread which keeps him from harm inside a fiery furnace evokes the story of Shadrach, Meshach, and Abednego in Daniel (3: 10–30); the Holy Sacrament's curing of a demoniac recalls Jesus's similar feat in Mark (5: 1–16); and the multiplication of some twenty consecrated wafers—or Hosts—into enough to serve almost 600 people obviously recalls Jesus's miraculous feeding of the multitude of 5,000 with only "five loaves, and two fishes" (Matthew 14:15–21). (Interestingly, the multiplying Hosts was accomplished by St. John Bosco, 1815–1888, who, in his youth, had been a magician [Cruz 1987, 208]!)

Many of the Eucharistic miracle stories have a suspiciously similar plot, which suggests derivation. For example, at least three stories—from Lanciano, Italy, eighth century; Regensburg, Germany, 1257; and Bolsena, Italy, 1263—concern a priest who had doubts about the reality of transubstantiation. When he spoke the words of Consecration, the Host was suddenly transformed into flesh and/or the wine became visible blood (Cruz 1987, 3–7; 59–62).

As another example, several tales—from Alatri, Italy, 1228; Santarem, Portugal, early thirteenth century; and Offida, Italy, 1280—feature a woman who kept the Host in her mouth so she could make off with it and, as instructed by some occultist, transform it into a love potion. Subsequently, the Host was turned into flesh (Cruz 1987, 30–37; 70–83), and in one instance it also issued a mysterious light (Cruz 1987, 38–46).

At least two anti-Semitic tales—one from Paris, France, 1290; and one from Brussels, Belgium, 1370—involve a Jew or Jews illicitly acquiring a consecrated wafer and stabbing it with a knife, whereupon blood spurted forth in triumph over their mocking disbelief (Cruz 1987,

63–65; 112–122).[3] In the latter tale there are even conflicting accounts of the Jews' fate: one says they were burned at the stake, the other that they were banished from the area. Such *variants*—as folklorists call them—are a "defining characteristic of folklore," since oral transmission naturally produces differing versions of the same tale (Brunvand 1978, 7).

Turin 'Miracle'

The story of "the miracle of Turin" begins just before the middle of the year 1453 at a church in Exilles (then in the French Dauphinate), according to a parchment that I personally examined at the Turin city archives (Valle n.d.). Reportedly, some men (two soldiers, in popular legend [Cruz 1987, 145]) had come from a war between the French Savoys and the Piedmontese, pillaged a church, and then loaded a sackful of plunder—including a silver reliquary with a sacred Host—upon a mule. They made their way via Susa, Avigliana, and Rivoli to Turin, but after the beast passed through the city gate, it halted in front of the church of San Silvestro and fell to the ground. Out of the pack tumbled the Host—"the true body of Christ"—and it miraculously ascended into the air, shining "like the sun." The bishop, Ludovico Romagno, was summoned along with the clergy, whereupon they discovered the reliquary on the ground and "the body of the Lord in the air with great Radiant splendor." The bishop knelt and brought out a chalice into which the Host descended, thence being transported to "the doorway of the Cathedral."

The parchment, signed only by a ducal official, nevertheless lists the names of several witnesses and notes that "after completion of the new cathedral" the Host is to rest therein and to be the subject of an annual octave (an eight-day event) in commemoration of the "miracle" (Valle n.d.).

Unfortunately, there are problems with the document, although it is certainly consistent with a parchment of the fifteenth or early sixteenth century.[4] Significantly, it is undated and merely bears in the heading the date of the reported event: "in the year 1453 on the 6 of June, a Thursday." Actually, the sixth was a Wednesday, only one of several indications that something is amiss. Another problem is the reference to the anticipated completion of the "new cathedral," presumably that of St. John the Baptist, which was not built until 1491–98 ("Turin" 2007).

Everything about the document indicates it is not original, including the fact that another undated one—with a similar text (including the erroneous "Thursday")—is known. Indeed, it is the latter whose text is reproduced in the official booklet published with the imprimatur of the Metropolitan Curia of Turin. However, this document is noted as "presently missing" and—lest it be thought to have been the original— is described as a "sixteenth-century text" (*Il Miracolo* 1997, 55). Moreover, although the two documents include many similarities, there are differences in wording and detail. For instance, the published document specifically mentions the Cathedral of St. John the Baptist by name, and the respective lists of witnesses' names show evidence of garbling. (For example, "Michaele Burry" is given in the parchment versus "Michel Muri" in the published document; only one of the eleven names is exactly the same, and the published document omits a name. The list in Cruz [1987] is different still.)

Despite the late, differing versions and the apparent lack of a true original—all of which inspires skepticism—the copies themselves nevertheless indicate there was, at least at some point, a narrative and a list of names of alleged eyewitnesses to some occurrence. But what was it?

An Explanation

The texts suggest that it may well have been some celestial event, the supposed Host being described as "in the air with great Radiant splendor" and "shining like the sun" (see Figure 1). The accounts say the event occurred "at hour 20" (Valle n.d.; *Il Miracolo* 1997, 55), but the printed text has an editorial insertion clarifying that it was "between the hours 16 and 17"—i.e., between four and five o'clock in the afternoon (*Il Miracolo* 1997, 55). Therefore the duration was apparently less than one hour. On the other hand, the event obviously lasted long enough for residents to fetch the Bishop and clergy, so it was too long for, say, a meteor.

That it was described as "shining like the sun" suggests to me it could have been a phenomenon known as a "mock sun" (or "sun dog"), that is, a parhelion. Parhelia can appear as very bright patches in the sky and are among the various ice-crystal refraction effects that include halos, arcs, solar pillars, and other atmospheric phenomena (Greenler 1999, 23–64).

I posed the question of the mystery occurrence to Major James McGaha (USAF, retired), who is not only an experienced pilot and noted UFO expert but also director of the Grasslands Observatory in Tucson, Arizona. He conducted a computer search of the sky for the place, date, and time of the occurrence. He found nothing of an astronomical nature that might have caused such an effect. (For example, there was

Figure 1. Painting of "the Miracle of Turin" by Bartolomeo Garavaglia in the Church of Corpus Domini, Turin, Italy (Photo by Joe Nickell).

no conjunction of planets, and the moon—a new moon—would have been invisible [McGaha 2008].)

He agreed with my suggestion that a parhelion-type phenomenon could be consistent with the "miracle of Turin." That is especially likely in light of the celestial object being reported as "over the surrounding houses" and "shining, as a second sun" ("Eucharistic" 2007)—an apt description if the phenomenon were indeed a mock sun. A parhelion could well last for the duration reported and would be most likely to appear when the sun was relatively low in the sky, observed McGaha (2008).

He considered one other possibility given that there was a question of the date. If the event did occur on June 6 but three years later, in 1456, the celestial object could convincingly be identified as Halley's Comet.

In any event, what might have happened is that the witnessing of a genuine, sensational occurrence was seen as miraculous—a "sign"—by superstitious folk and clergy, the latter interpreting it as the radiant body of Christ in the sky. This could have prompted the Bishop to hold aloft not only a chalice but also a Host, and as the phenomenon soon ceased to be visible, the belief was that the celestial light was absorbed by the wafer. According to this scenario, it was this "miraculous" Host that was displayed. (It was thus kept until 1584 when the Holy see ordered it consumed so as "not to oblige God to maintain an eternal miracle by keeping the Host always perfect and pure" (qtd. in Cruz 1987, 147).

This celestial incident, witnessed by various persons, might then have been grafted by the process of folklore onto a somewhat similar tale, like one set in Paris in 1274 (Cruz 1987, 63). Or it could have been confabulated—in the manner of the Roswell UFO crash myth (McAndrew 1997)—and enhanced by faulty perceptions and memories, together with the impulse to create a pious legend.

Such religious legends are often called *belief tales* because they are intentionally grafted "to give credence to folk beliefs" (Brunvand 1978, 106–108). Indeed, Cruz (1987, 145) states revealingly that "At the time of the miracle of Turin, the faith of the people had grown feeble, and it is thought God wanted to give a sign to arouse them from their apathy." The miracle, she states, "effected the desired change."

Arguing in favor of this hypothesis, I think, is the allegorical nature of the Turin narrative—a dramatic tale in its own right, and an even more profoundly Christian one if seen as allegory of the life, death, and resurrection of Jesus. Consider, for example that similar to Jesus's emerging from exile (Matthew 2: 13–15), in the Turin-miracle narrative the Corpus Domini ("Body of Christ") is placed on a mule and led from Exilles into

Turin (which is to become known as "the city of the Holy sacrament" [*Il Miracolo* 1997, 32]). Jesus's Last Supper (Matthew 26: 17–30) is evoked by the wafer of communion bread, which has been spilled.

This (tradition says) happened between two robbers, like Jesus's crucifixion, which occurred between two thieves (Matthew 27:38). And just as Jesus bodily arose from his tomb (Matthew 28: 1–7) and was "carried up into heaven" (Mark 24:51), the "Body of Christ" emerged from its reliquary (a container for holy remains) and ascended into the sky, radiant like the sun, as Jesus came to be (says John 9:5) "the light of the world." The subsequent descent of the Holy Host into the chalice obviously symbolizes the gift of the Eucharist to Christianity—a theme common to all of the Eucharistic "miracle" tales.

Acknowledgments

The following people were extremely helpful in this investigation: At CFI, Libraries Director Timothy Binga and Art Director Lisa Hutter; in Turin, Stefano Bagnasco, Andrea Ferrero, Claudio Pastore, Beatrice Mautino, and Mario Tomatis; and, accompanying me to Lackawanna, my wife, Diana Harris.

Notes

1. For an updated discussion of the Shroud of Turin see Nickell 2007, 122–179.

2. Another version of Luke is in Codex Bezae (Price 2003, 298).

3. In the first instance the man is not stated to be a Jew, but it is implied by his being a "non-Christian" and, stereotypically, a "pawnbroker" and is further indicated by the similar tale specifically involving Jews assembled in a synagogue.

4. Examination with a 10x Bausch & Lomb illuminated coddington magnifier reveals that the parchment's text was penned with a quill in an ink that has the appearance of an age-browned (oxidized) iron-gallotannate variety and is in an italic hand known as *cancellaresca*—i.e., "chancery" script—because it was widely disseminated by scribes of the Papal Chancery in the fifteenth and sixteenth centuries (Whalley 1984, 22, 41, 181; Nickell 2003, 123, 131, 140).

References

Borg, Marcus J., and John Dominic Crossan. 2006. *The Last Week*. New York: Harper San Francisco.

Brunvand, Jan Harold. 1978. *The Study of American Folklore: An Introduction*, 2nd ed., New York: W.W. Norton.

Cruz, Joan Carroll. 1987. *Eucharistic Miracles and Eucharistic Phenomena in the Lives of the Saints*. Rockford, Illinois: Tan Books and Publishers.

Dummelow, J.R., ed. 1951. *A Commentary on the Holy Bible by Various Writers*. New York: Macmillan.

The Eucharistic Miracles of the World. 2007. Available online at www.thereal presence.org/eucharist/mir/engl_mir.htm; accessed September 7, 2007.

Greenler, Robert. 1999. *Rainbows, Halos, and Glories*. Milwaukee, Wisconsin: Peanut Butter Publishing, 23–64.

Il Miracolo di Torino. 1997. Turin, Italy: Metropolitan Curia of Turin.

McAndrew, James. 1997. *The Roswell Report: Case Closed*. Washington, D.C.: U.S. Government Printing Office.

McGaha, James E. 2008. Personal communication, February 1.

Nickell, Joe. 2003. *Pen, Ink & Evidence*. New Castle, Delaware: Oak Knoll Press.

————. 2007. *Relics of the Christ*. Lexington, Ky.: University Press of Kentucky.

Price, Robert M. 2003. *The Incredible Shrinking Son of Man: How Reliable Is the Gospel Tradition?* Amherst, N.Y.: Prometheus Books.

Shapcote, Emily Mary. 1877. *Legends of the Blessed Sacrament,Gathered from . . . .* London: Burns and Oates.

Stravinskas, Peter M.J. 2002. *Catholic Dictionary*, revised. Huntington, Indiana: Our Sunday Visitor Publishing Division.

Turin Cathedral. 2007. Wikipedia, the free encyclopedia. Available online at http://en.wikipedia.org/wiki/Cathedral_of_Saint_John_the_Baptist_(Turin); accessed September 7, 2007.

Valle, Thomaso. N.d. Parchment account of 1453 "miracle" of Turin in the Historical Archives of the City of Turin (part of archive catalog no. 936, in loose papers collection); personally examined October 14, 2004.

Whalley, Joyce Irene. 1984. *The Student's Guide to Western Calligraphy*. Boulder, Colorado: Shambhala Publications.

Grilled-Cheese Madonna

Since it came to light in 2004, it has become the quintessential holy image to appear on an item of food: the face, many say, of the Virgin Mary on a grilled-cheese sandwich. While it has sparked little piety—the Catholic church has not sanctioned it as divine—it has become the subject of controversy and ridicule and has even suffered insinuations of fakery. I once had custody of the curious item, and I was actually able to photograph and examine the image under magnification (Figures 1–2). Here are my findings.

Background

The image reportedly appeared ten years earlier in the Hollywood, Florida, home of Gregg and Diana Duyser. Mrs. Duyser, fifty-two, said she had grilled the sandwich without butter or oil and had just taken a bite when she noticed—staring back at her—the image of a woman's face in the toasting pattern. She perceived it as the face of "The Virgin Mary, Mother of God" and, placing it in a plastic box with cotton balls, kept it enshrined on her night stand.

Duyser was impressed that the sandwich never molded. However, toast and hardened cheese that are kept dry naturally resist molding.

The Duysers received $28,000 when they auctioned the sandwich on the Internet site eBay. The site had initially pulled the item—which supposedly broke its policy of not allowing "Listings that are intended as jokes"—but the couple insisted that the item was neither a joke nor a hoax. Soon the "'Virgin Mary' sandwich" was back, attracting bids. It was purchased by an online casino—Golden Palace.com—whose CEO, Richard Rowe, stated that he intended to use the sandwich to raise funds for charity ("Virgin Mary" 2004).

Simulacra

The image-bearing sandwich received—possibly outdistanced—the notoriety accorded other sacred food icons. They include Maria Rubio's famous 1977 tortilla that bore the face of Jesus, also in the pattern of skillet burns; a giant forkful of spaghetti pictured on a billboard in which some perceived the likeness of Christ; and the image of Mother Teresa discovered on a cinnamon bun (see Nickell 2004).

Queried by the Associated Press during the holy-grilled-cheese brouhaha, I explained that such images are nothing more than evidence of the human ability—termed *pareidolia*—to interpret essentially random patterns, such as ink blots or pictures in clouds, as recognizable images. The most famous example is the face of the Man in the Moon.

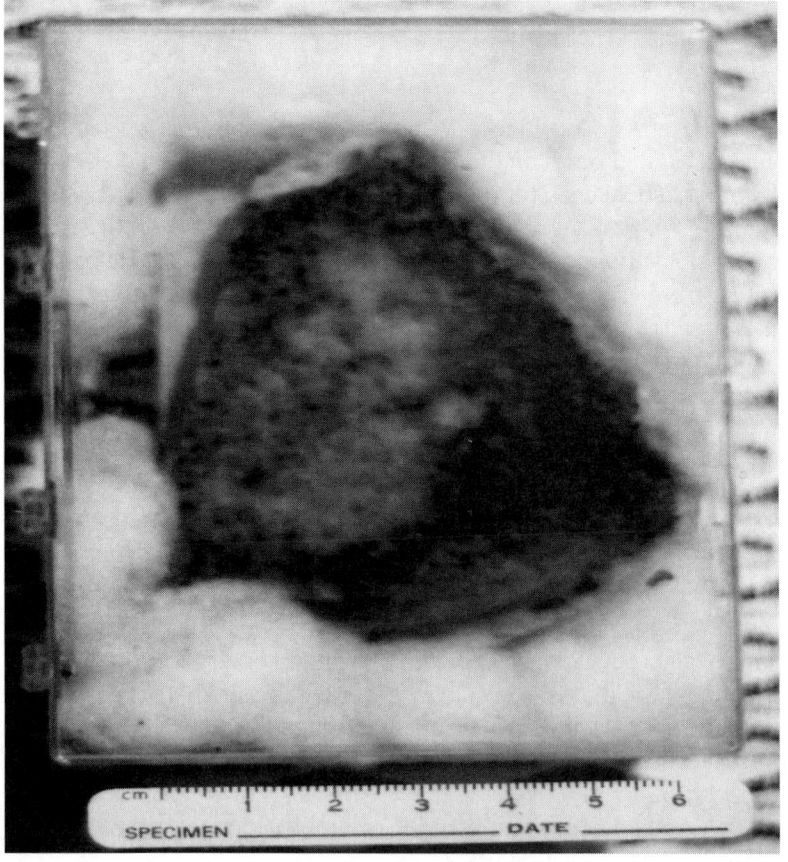

Figure 1. The famous face-bearing grilled-cheese sandwich has been kept in a plastic case since its creation in 1994. (Forensic scale added; photo by Joe Nickell)

Perceived pictures of this type are called *simulacra*, and many are interpreted as religious images (a female face becoming "Mary," for example). These are perhaps most often associated with Catholic or Orthodox traditions, wherein there is a special emphasis on icons or other holy images (Nickell 2004; Thompson 2004).

In the wake of the grilled-cheese image came others, one on a fish stick hailed as "the son of Cod" ("It's" 2004), another a pair of images on a pancake. A woman interpreted the latter duo as Jesus and Mary, while her mother, the actual flapjack flipper, thought it resembled a bedouin and Santa Claus (Nohlgren 2004). The grilled-cheese icon even helped inspire an entire book: called *Madonna of the Toast* (Poole 2007), it treats both "Secular Sightings" (e.g., Myrtle Young's famous collection of pictorial potato chips) and "Forms of Faith" (including the previously mentioned Mother Teresa "Nun Bun"—missing since it was stolen in 2005).

A Hoax?

The Duysers' grilled-cheese Madonna was lampooned on Penn and Teller's *Bullshit!* series on the Showtime Network (2006) and elsewhere by other debunkers (Stollznow 2006). Some of them found clever ways to make fake images on toast. One method involved a custom cast-iron skillet molded with Jesus's face, another a yeast extract used to paint pictures on bread before toasting (Poole 2007, 88–89). A Holy Toast!™ "miracle bread stamper" was even marketed in 2006.

But was the image due to possible trickery, as some implied? The rush to suggest fakery antecedent to inquiry is a most unfortunate approach. It is certainly not the method of a serious, intellectually honest investigation.

As it happens, I was able to examine the grilled cheese in question in 2005. I had custody of it for the better part of a day, January 14, courtesy of its Las Vegas-based owners who loaned it to the Penn and Teller show's producer who in turn entrusted it to me. I was in Las Vegas to tape segments for that popular program, the timing of which coincided with the James Randi Educational Foundation's annual conference, The Amaz!ng Meeting 3 (held at the Stardust Resort & Casino). There, I shared the framed pop icon with other skeptics who eagerly posed with it, including Michael Shermer and Steve Shaw (aka the mentalist Banachek). No one thought the image looked like the Virgin Mary (as her visage is imagined in art); instead some suggested it resembled Gretta Garbo, Marlena Dietrich, or other celebrities.

Eventually I retired to a suite where I could study the controversial

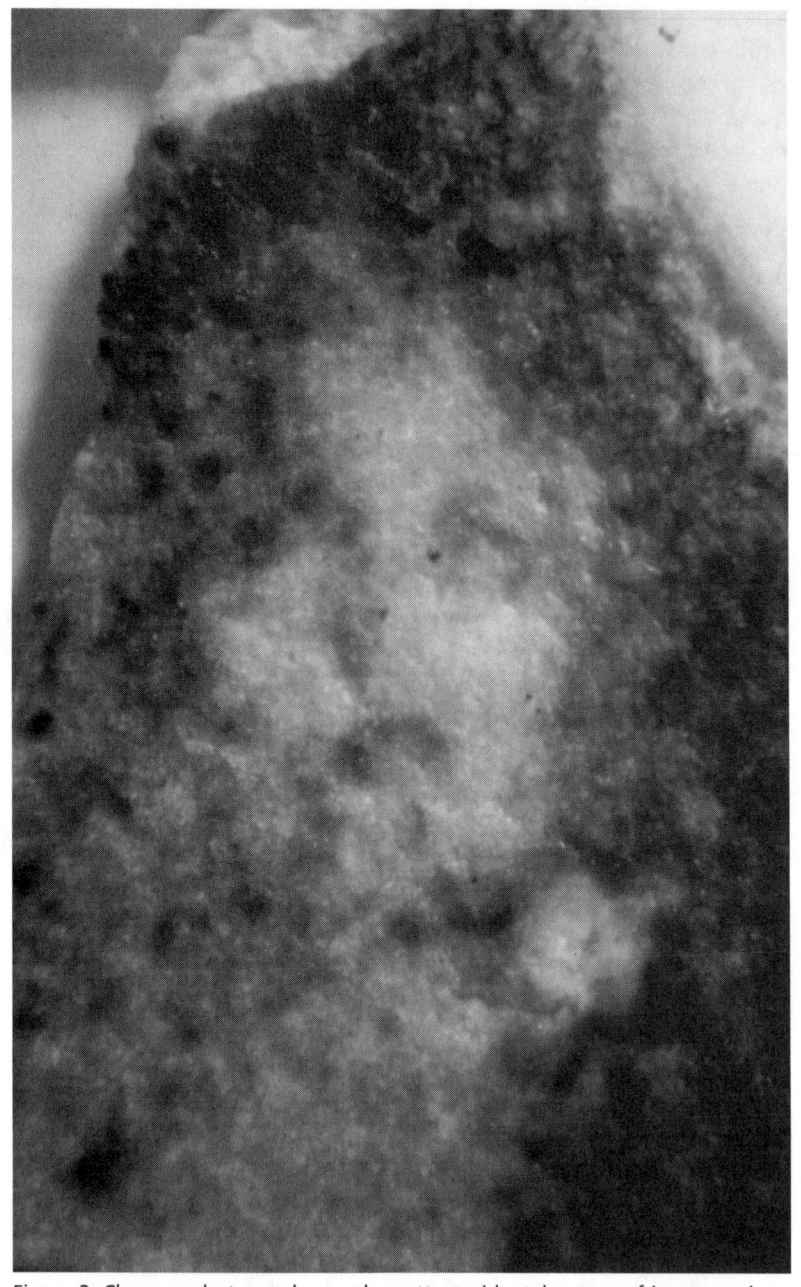

Figure 2. Close-up photograph reveals spotty, accidental nature of image: a simulacrum. (Photo by Joe Nickell)

sandwich. It was in what appeared to be its original plastic box, surrounded with cotton balls, and set in a deep frame. I placed a forensic centimeter scale thereon and photographed the sandwich using a 35mm camera and close-up lenses (again, see Figures 1–2). I also examined it macroscopically, using a 10x Bausch & Lomb illuminated coddington magnifier.

I observed that the surface had a spotty, heat-blistered appearance (again, see Figure 2). The spots making up "eyes," "nose," and "mouth" are similar to those elsewhere on the toasted bread. There was no apparent difference or incongruity with regard to hue, sheen, form, or indeed other characteristic. That is to say, there were no facial areas that seemed more linear or in any way drawn or added (as by, say, use of a woodburning tool or by any of various other means I considered). Therefore, it is consistent with a genuine (accidentally produced) simulacrum rather than a faked one.

Moreover, a careful close-up look at the "face" reveals it to be far less perfect than it may at first sight appear. (Those who suggest that hoaxing may have been involved, please take notice.) The features really consist only of some squiggles, a fact perhaps best appreciated by turning the picture ninety-degrees. The nostrils are missing, yet the mind—"recognizing" a face—fills them in. Again, there is a pronounced extraneous, curved mark on the lady's right cheek, yet the mind tends helpfully to filter it out (or perhaps interpret it as, say, a curl of hair). In short, the image seems a rather typical simulacrum.

Nevertheless, Diana Duyser certainly acts as if she believes that the "Virgin Mary" image on the grilled cheese is, as she says, "a miracle." No longer owning the sandwich, she has had its image tattooed onto one of her ample breasts (pictured in Poole 2007, 86). She thus demonstrates that with simulacra, belief—as well as beauty—is often in the eye of the beholder.

References

It's the son of Cod. 2004. *The Daily Telegraph*. Available online at http://dailytelegraph. news.com.au/story.jsp?sectionid=1260&storyid=2282668; accessed November 29, 2004.

Nickell, Joe. 2004. Rorshach icons. *Skeptical Inquirer's* 28:6 (November/December), 15–17.

Nohlgren, Stephen. 2004. Flapjack Jesus flips along eBay. *St. Petersburg Times*. Available online at www.sptimes.com/2007/11/20/state/Flapjack_Jesus_flips_.shtml; accessed November 21, 2004.

Penn & Teller: Bullshit! The Complete Third Season. 2006. Three-volume DVD set, produced by Showtime. Vol. 3, incl. "Signs from Heaven."

Poole, Buzz. 2007. *Madonna of the Toast*. New York: Mark Batty Publisher.

Stollznow, Karen. 2008. Merchandising God: The pope tart. *Skeptical Inquirer* 32:3 (May/June), 45–51.

Thompson, Carolyn. 2004. Expert explains grilled cheese "miracle" (AP). Available online at www.newsday.com/news/local/wire/my-bc-ny--cheesymiracle-exp1117nov17,0, 65619...; accessed November 17, 2004.

"Virgin Mary" sandwich. 2004. Available online at www.cnn.com/2004/us/11/23/ebay.sandwich.ap/index.html; accessed November 23.

Undercover Among the Spirits

Camp Chesterfield is a notorious spiritualist enclave of Chesterfield, Indiana. Dubbed "the Coney Island of spiritualism," it has been the target of many exposés, notably a book by a confessed fraudulent medium published in 1976. A quarter century later I decided to see if the old deceptions were still being practiced at the camp; naturally my visit was both unannounced and undercover.

The Background

Modern spiritualism began in 1848 with the schoolgirl pranks of Maggie and Katie Fox in Hydesville, New York. Although four decades later the sisters confessed that their "spirit" rappings had been bogus, in the meantime the craze of allegedly communicating with the dead had spread across America, Europe, and beyond. At séances held in darkened rooms and theaters, "mediums" (those who supposedly contacted spirits for others) produced such phenomena as slate writing, table tipping, and "materializations" of spirit entities.

As adherents grew in number, spiritualist camp meetings began to be common, and some groups established permanent spiritualist centers.

Perhaps none developed such an unsavory reputation as Camp Chesterfield, which opened in 1891. Even today, spiritualist friends of mine roll their eyes accusatorially whenever Chesterfield's name is mentioned, and they are quick to point out that the camp is not chartered by the National Spiritualist Association of Churches. The introduction to an official history of Chesterfield (*Chesterfield Lives* 1986, 6), admits it is surprising the camp has survived, given its troubled past:

In fact, in its 100 years of recorded history, Camp Chesterfield has been "killed off" more than once! There have been cries of "fraud" and "fake" (and these

> were some of the nicer things we have been called!) and of course, the "exposés" came along with the regularity of a well-planned schedule. Oh yes! We have been damned and downed—but the fact remains that we must have been doing something right because: CHESTERFIELD LIVES!!

Be that as it may, the part about the exposés is certainly true.

A major exposé came in 1960 when two researchers—both sympathetic to spiritualism—arranged to film the supposed materialization of spirits. This was to occur under the mediumship of Edith Stillwell, who was noted for her multiple-figure spirit manifestations, and the séance was to be documented using see-in-the-dark technology. While the camera ran, luminous spectral figures took form and vanished near the medium's cabinet, but when the infrared film was processed the researchers saw that the ghosts were actually confederates dressed in luminous gauze, some of whom were recognizable as Chesterfield residents. They had not materialized and dematerialized but rather came and went through a secret door that led to an adjacent apartment (Keene 1976, 40; Christopher 1970, 174). One of the researchers, himself a devout spiritualist, was devastated by the evidence and railed against "the frauds, fakes and fantasies of the Chesterfield Spiritualist camp!" (O'Neill 1960).

An even more devastating exposé came in 1976 with the book *The Psychic Mafia* written by former Chesterfield medium M. Lamar Keene. Saying that money was "the name of the game" at Chesterfield, Keene detailed the many tricks used by mediums there which he dubbed "the Coney Island of Spiritualism." He told how "apports" (said to be materialized gifts from spirits) were purchased and hidden in readiness for the séance; how chiffon became "ectoplasm" (an imagined mediumistic substance); how sitters' questions written on slips of paper called billets were secretly read and then answered; how trumpets were made to float in the air with discarnate voices speaking through them; and how other tricks were accomplished to bilk credulous sitters (Keene 1976, 95–114).

Keene also told how the billets were shrewdly retained from the various public clairvoyant message services held at Chesterfield. Kept in voluminous files beneath the Cathedral, the billets—along with a medium's own private files and those shared by fellow scam artists—provided excellent resources for future readings.

There were other exposés of Camp Chesterfield. In 1985 a medium from there was making visits to Lexington, Kentucky, where he conducted dark-room materialization séances. He featured the production of apports, the floating-trumpet-with-spirit-voices feat, and something called "spirit precipitations on silk." To produce the latter, the sitters' "spirit guides" supposedly took ink from an open bottle and created their own small self-portraits on swatches of cloth the sitters held in their laps. I investigated when one sitter complained, suspecting fraud. Laboratory analyses by forensic analyst John F. Fischer revealed the presence of solvent stains (shown under argon laser light). A recipe for such productions given by Keene (1976, 110–111)—utilizing a solvent to transfer pictures from newspapers or magazines—enabled me to create similar "precipitations" (Nickell with Fischer 1988). The prepared swatches had obviously been switched for the blank ones originally shown.

Undercover

I had long wanted to visit Camp Chesterfield, and in the summer of 2001, following a trip to Kentucky to see my elderly mother and other family members, I decided to head north to Indiana to check out the notorious site.

Now, skeptics have never been welcome at Chesterfield. The late Mable Riffle, a medium who ran the camp from 1909 until her death in 1961 (*Chesterfield Lives*, 1986) dealt with them summarily. When she heard one couple using the f-word—*fraud*—she snarled, reports Keene (1976, 48), "We do not have that kind of talk here. Now you get your goddam ass off these hallowed grounds and don't ever come back!"

Another skeptic, a reporter named Rosie who had written a series of exposés and was banned from the grounds, had the nerve to return. Wearing a "fright wig," she got into one of Riffle's séances and when the "spirits" began talking through the trumpet the reporter began to demean them. According to Keene (1976, 48–49), Riffle recognized Rosie's voice immediately and went for her. "Grabbing the reporter by the back of the neck, she ushered her up a steep flight of stairs, kicking her in the rump on each step and cursing her with every profanity imaginable."

With these lessons in mind, I naturally did not want to be recognized at Chesterfield—not out of fear for my personal safety but so as to be able to observe unimpeded for as long as possible. When in my younger years I was a private investigator with an international detective agency, I generally used my own name and appearance and, for undercover jobs, I merely wore the attire that was appropriate for a forklift driver, steelworker, tavern waiter, or other "role" (Nickell 2001).

The same is true for several previous undercover visits to paranormal sites and gatherings (including a private spiritualistic circle which included table-tipping and other séances that I infiltrated in 2000). Since I am often the token skeptic on television talk shows and documentaries on the paranormal, I have naturally feared I might be recognized, but I rarely made any effort to disguise myself and usually had no problem.

However, for my stint at Camp Chesterfield, I felt special measures were called for so I decided to alter my appearance, shaving off my mustache (for the first time in over thirty years!), and replacing my coat-and-tie look with a T-shirt, suspenders, straw hat, and cane. I also adopted a pseudonym, "James Collins," after the name of one of Houdini's assistants. From July 19 to 23, "Jim," who seemed bereft at what he said was the recent death of his mother, limped up and down the grounds and spent nights at one of the camp's two hotels (devoid of such amenities as TV and air conditioning). The results were eye-opening, involving a panoply of discredited spiritualist practices that seemed little changed from when they were revealed in *The Psychic Mafia*.

Billet Reading

I witnessed three versions of the old billet scam: one done across the table from me during a private reading, and two performed for church audiences, one of them accomplished with the medium blindfolded.

The first situation—with the medium working one-on-one with the client—involves getting a peek at the folded slip while the person is distracted. (Magicians call this *misdirection*.) For instance, while the medium directs the sitter's attention, say by pointing to some numerological scribblings (as were offered in my case), she can surreptitiously open the billet in her lap with a flick of the thumb of her other hand and quickly glimpse the contents. As expected, the alleged clairvoyant knew exactly what was penned on my slip—the names of four persons who had "passed into spirit" and two questions—but did not know that the people were fictitious.

One aspect of the reading, which was held in the séance room of her cottage, was particularly amusing. At times she would turn to her right—as if acknowledging the presence of an invisible entity—and say "Yes I will." This was a seeming acknowledgment of some message she supposedly received from a spirit, which she was to impart to me. I paid the medium thirty dollars cash and considered it a bargain—although not in the way the spiritualist would no doubt have hoped.

At both of the billet readings I attended that were conducted for audiences (one in a chapel, the other in the cathedral), a volunteer stood inside the doorway and handed each of us a slip of paper. Printed instructions at the top directed us to "Please address your billet to one or more loved ones in spirit, giving first and last names. Ask one or more questions and sign your full name."

On the first occasion I made a point of seeming uncertain about how to fold the paper and was told that it was to be simply doubled over and creased; if it was done otherwise, I was told strictly, the medium would not read it. I did not ask why, since I tried to seem as credulous as possible, but in fact I knew that there were two reasons. First, of course, the billets needed to be easy to open with a flick of the thumb, and second, it was essential that they all look alike. The reason for the latter condition lay in the method employed: After the slips were gathered in a collection plate and dumped atop the lectern (where they could not be seen from our vantage point) the medium would pick one up and hold it to his or her forehead while divining its contents. The trick involves secretly glancing down at an open billet. A sitter who had closed his slip in a distinctive way (such as by pleating it or folding it into a triangle) might notice that the billet being shown was not the one apparently being viewed clairvoyantly.

The insistence on how the paper must be folded indicated trickery. And that was confirmed for me at one session through my writing the names of non-existent loved ones and signing with my pseudonym. From near the back of the chapel I acknowledged the medium's announcement that he was "getting the Collins family." After revealing the bogus names I had written, he gave me an endearing message from my supposedly departed mother that answered a question I had addressed to her on the billet. However, my mother was actually among the living and, of course, not named Collins.

The other public billet reading I attended was part of a Gala Service held in the Cathedral. The medium placed adhesive strips over her eyes followed by a scarf tied in blindfold fashion. This is obviously supposed to prove that the previously described method of billet reading was not employed, but according to Keene (1976, 45), who performed the same feat, "The secret here was the old mentalist standby: the peek down the side of the nose." He adds: "No matter how securely the eyes are blindfolded, it's always possible to get enough of a gap to read material held close to the body." Unfortunately, at this reading my billet was not among those chosen, so there were no special communications from the non-existent persons whose names I had penned.

Spirit Writing

Another feat practiced by at least three mediums at Chesterfield is called "spirit card writing." This descends from the old slate effects that were common during the heyday of spiritualism, whereby (in a typical effect) alleged otherworldly writing mysteriously appeared on the inner sur-faces of a pair of slates that were bound together (Nickell 2000). In the modern form (which exists in several variants), blank cards are placed in a basket along with an assortment of pens, colored pencils, etc. After a suitable invocation, each of the cards is seen typically to bear a sitter's name surrounded by the names of his "spirit guides" or other entities and possibly a drawing or other artwork. The sitter keeps the card as a tangible "proof" of spirit power.

At Chesterfield one afternoon I attempted to sign up for a private card-writing séance later that evening at the home of a prominent medium (who also advertises other feats including "pictures on silk"). When that session proved to be filled, I decided to try to "crash" the event and soon hit on a subterfuge. I placed the autograph of "Jim Collins" on the sign-in sheet for the *following* week, then showed up at the appointed time for the current séance a few hours later. I milled about with the prospective sitters, and then we were all ushered into the séance room in the medium's bungalow.

So far so good. Unfortunately when he read off the signees' names and I was unaccounted for, I had some explaining to do. I insisted I had signed the sheet and let him discover the "error" I had made. Then, suitably repentant and deeply disappointed, I implored him to allow me to stay, noting that there was more than one extra seat. Of course, if the affair were bogus, and the cards prepared in advance, I could not be permitted to participate. Not surprisingly I was not, being given the lame excuse (by another medium, a young woman, who was sitting in on the session) that the medium needed to prepare for the séance by "meditating" on each sitter's name. (I wondered which of the two types of mediums she was: one of the "shut-eyes," simple believers who fancy that they receive psychic impressions, or one of the "open mediums," who acknowledge their deceptions within the secret frater-nity [Keene 1976, 23].) Even without my admission fee, I estimate the medium grossed approximately $450.

The next day I sought out one of the sitters who consoled me over my not having been accepted for the séance. She showed me her card, which bore a scattering of names like "Gray Wolf" in various colors of felt-pen handprinting—all appearing to me on brief inspection to have been done by one person. The other side of the card bore a picture (somewhat resembling a Japanese art print) that she thought had also been produced by spirits, although I do not know exactly what was claimed by the medium. I did examine the picture with the small lens on my Swiss army knife, which revealed the telltale pattern of dots from the halftone printing process. The woman seemed momentarily discomfited when I showed her this and indeed acknowledged that the whole thing seemed hard to believe, but she stated that she simply *chose* to believe. I nodded understandingly; I was not there to argue with her.

'Direct Voice'

My most memorable—and unbelievable—experience at Camp Chesterfield involved a spirit materialization séance I attended at a medium's cottage on a Sunday morning. Such offerings are not scheduled in the camp's guidebook but are rather advertised via a sign-in book, and, perhaps an accompanying poster, on the medium's porch. As my previous experience showed, it behooved one to keep abreast of the various offerings around the village. So I was out early in the morning, hobbling with my cane up and down the narrow lanes. Soon, a small poster caught my eye: "Healing Séance with Apports." It being just after 6:00 A.M., and the streets silent, I quietly stepped onto the porch and signed up for the 10:00 A.M. session.

At the appointed time seven of us had gathered and the silver-haired medium ushered us into the séance room, which she promptly secured against light leakage, placing a rolled-up throw rug at the bottom of the outer door and another rolled cloth to seal the top, and closing a curtain across an interior door. She collected twenty-five dollars from each attendee and then, after a brief prayer, launched into the healing service. This consisted of a "pep talk" (as she termed it) followed by a brief session with each participant in which she clasped the person's hands and imparted supposed healing energies.

It eventually came time for the séance. A pair of tin spirit trumpets standing on the floor by the medium's desk suggested we might experience "direct voice," by which spirits supposedly speak, the trumpets often being used to amplify the vocalizations. The medium began by turning off the lamps and informing us that "dark is light." Soon, in the utter blackness, the voices came, seeming to be speaking in turn through one of the trumpets. Keene (1976, 104–108) details various means of producing "levitating" trumpets, complete with luminescent bands around them "so that the sitters could see them whirling around the room, hovering in space, or sometimes swinging back and forth in rhythm with a hymn." But here, however, we were left to our imaginations. Mine suggested to me that the medium was not even bothering to use the large trumpet, which might prove tiresome, but may have been utilizing a small tin megaphone—another trick described by Keene.

Some mediums were better at pretending direct voice than others; sometimes, according to one critic, "All the spirit voices sounded exactly like the medium . . ." (Keene 1976, 122). Such was the case at my séance. The first voice sounded just like the medium using exaggerated enunciation to simulate an "Ascended Master" (who urged the rejection of negativity); another sounded just like the medium adopting the craggy voice of "Black Elk" (with a message about having respect for the Earth); and still another sounded just like the medium using a perky little-girl voice to conjure up "Miss Poppy" (supposedly one of the medium's "joy guides").

At the end of the séance, after the lights were turned back on, one of the trumpets was lying on its side on the floor, as if dropped there by the spirits—or, as I thought, simply tipped over by the medium. Finally, we were invited up to get our "apports."

Apports

Supposedly materialized or teleported gifts from the spirits, apports appear at some séances under varying conditions—sometimes tumbling out of a spirit trumpet, for example. Keene (1976, 108) says those at Camp Chesterfield were typically "worthless trinkets" such as broaches or rings often "bought cheap in bulk." One medium specialized in "spirit jewels" (colored glass) while another apported arrowheads; special customers might receive something "more impressive." Camp Chesterfield instructed its apport mediums to ". . . *please ask your guides* to bring articles of equal worth to each sitter and not to bring only one of such articles as are usually in pairs (earrings or cufflinks, for instance)" (quoted from "The Medium's Handbook" by Keene 1976, 63).

At our séance the apports were specimens of hematite, which (like many other stones) has a long tradition of alleged healing and other powers (Kunz 1913). The shiny, steel-gray mineral had obviously been tumbled (mechanically polished), as indicated by surface characteristics shown by stereomicroscopic examination, and was indistinguishable from specimens purchased in shops that sell such New Age talismans.

The medium handed each of us one of the seven stones after picking it up with a tissue and noting with delight our reaction at discovering it was icy cold! This was a nice touch, I thought, imparting an element of unusualness as if somehow consistent with having been materialized from the Great Beyond—although probably only kept by the medium in her freezer until just before the séance when it was likely transferred to a thermos jar. We were told that each apport was attuned to that sitter's own energy "vibrations" and that no one else should ever be permitted to touch it. If someone did, we were warned, it would become "only a stone."

I left Camp Chesterfield on the morning of my fifth day there, after first taking photographs around the village. As I reflected on my experiences, things seemed to have changed little from the time Keene wrote about in *The Psychic Mafia*. Indeed the deceptions harkened back to the days of Houdini and beyond—actually, all the way back to 1848 when the Fox sisters launched the spiritualist craze with their schoolgirl tricks.

Acknowledgments

I am grateful to Brant Abrahamson of Brookfield, Illinois, who was prompted by my investigations of spiritualism to send me some materials he obtained while stopping at Camp Chesterfield during a trip. The materials helped seal my resolve to visit the site.

References

Christopher, Milbourne. 1970. *ESP, Seers & Psychics*. New York: Thomas Y. Crowell Co.

Keene, M. Lamar. 1976. *The Psychic Mafia*. Reprinted Amherst, N.Y.: Prometheus Books, 1997.

Kunz, George Frederick. 1913. *The Curious Lore of Precious Stones*; reprinted New York: Dover, 1971, 6, 80–81.

Nickell, Joe, with John F. Fischer. 1988. *Secrets of the Supernatural*. Buffalo, N.Y.: Prometheus Books.

———. 2000. Spirit painting, part II. *Skeptical Briefs* 10:2 (June), 9–11.

———.2001. Adventures of a Paranormal Investigator, in Paul Kurtz, ed., *Skeptical Odysseys*. Amherst, N.Y.: Prometheus Books, 219–232.

O'Neill, Tom. 1960. Quoted in Keene 1976, 40, and Christopher 1970, 175.

Searching for Vampire Graves

Given the ubiquitousness of vampires, those undead beings who are driven by bloodlust (and who thrive in movies like 2008's popular *Twilight*), it should not be surprising that historically there have been instances of reputed vampirism in the United States, notably in New England. And today there is a veritable vampire industry in New Orleans. I have investigated these cultural trends on site, tracking the legendary creatures to their very graves.

New England

New England has always been an admixture of both austere skepticism and passionate superstition. Vampire legends lurk in the latter. According to one vampirologist, "The presence in New England of a strongly rooted vampire mythology is something of an enigma to folklorists. There is quite simply no other area in all of North America with such wealth of vampire lore" (Rondina 2008, 165).

One of the best known examples is the case of nineteen-year-old Mercy Lena Brown in Exeter, Rhode Island, in 1892—a case that supposedly influenced Bram Stoker, author of *Dracula* (1897). As Katherine Ramsland (2002, 18) concisely tells the story:

> George Brown lost his wife and then his eldest daughter. One of his sons, Edwin, returned and once again became ill, so George exhumed the bodies of his wife and daughters. The wife and first daughter had decomposed, but Mercy's body—buried for three months—was fresh and turned sideways in the coffin, and blood dripped from her mouth. They cut out her heart, burned it, and dissolved the ashes in a medicine for Edwin to drink. However, he also died, and Mercy Brown became known as Exeter's vampire.

Accounts of the exhumation in the *Providence Journal* of March 19 and 21, 1892, acknowledge that the Browns died of consumption (tuberculosis). They do not mention the corpse of Lena (as she was actually known) being turned on its side or blood dripping from the mouth. The exhumation was conducted by a young Harold Metcalf, MD, from the city of Wickford. "Dr. Metcalf reports the body in a state of natural decomposition, with nothing exceptional existing," stated the *Journal*. "When the doctor removed the heart and the liver from the body a quantity of blood dripped therefrom, but this he said was just what might be expected from a similar examination of almost any person after the same length of time from disease." The article added, "The heart and liver were cremated by the attendants" ("Exhumed" 1892).

A follow-up article ("Vampire" 1892) noted that the heart's blood was "clotted and decomposed . . . just what might be expected at that stage of decomposition." The correspondent acknowledged the custom of an afflicted person consuming the ashes to effect a cure, stating, "In this case the doctor does not know if this latter remedy was resorted to or not, and he only knows from hearsay how ill the son Edwin is, never having been called to attend him."

And so ends "Unarguably the best known incident of historical vampirism in America," indeed the story of "The Last Vampire" (Rondina 2008, 83, 99). However, there are many other reported cases typically involving consumption. The victim's lethargy, pale appearance, coughing of blood, and contagiousness all suggested to the superstitious the result of a "vampire's parasitic kiss" (Citro 1994, 71).

The Demon Vampire

In 2008 I went in search of vampire cases in Vermont. Apparently the earliest reported vampire incident took place in Manchester in 1793. Four years earlier, Captain Isaac Burton—a deacon in the congregational church—wed Rachel Harris. Judge John S. Pettibone (1786–1872) picks up the story:

> She was, to use the words of one who was well acquainted with her, "a fine, healthy, beautiful girl." Not long after they were married she went into a decline and after a year or so she died of consumption. Capt. Burton after a year or more married Hulda Powel, daughter of Esquire Powel by his first wife. Hulda was a very healthy, good-looking girl, not as handsome as his first wife. She became ill soon after they were married and when she was in the last stages of consumption, a strange infatuation took possession of the minds of the connections and friends of the family. They were induced to believe that if the vitals of the first

wife could be consumed by being burned in a charcoal fire it would effect a cure of the sick second wife. Such was the strange delusion that they disinterred the first wife who had been buried about three years. They took out the liver, heart, and lungs, what remained of them, and burned them to ashes on the blacksmith's forge of Jacob Mead. Timothy Mead officiated at the altar in the sacrifice to the Demon Vampire who it was believed was still sucking the blood of the then living wife of Captain Burton. It was the month of February and good sleighing. Such was the excitement that from five hundred to one thousand people were present. This account was furnished me by an eye witness of the transaction.

Not only is Judge Pettibone's informant unnamed, but his manuscript (which still exists in the Manchester Historical Society [Harwood 2008]) is of uncertain date, although penned sometime between 1857 and 1872 (*Proceedings* 1930, 147). I located a Burton family history (Holman 1926) that makes no mention of the vampire tale but does confirm the sequence of marriages and deaths. (Captain Burton married Rachel Harris on March 8, 1789, and she died on February 1, 1790. He married Hulda Powell on January 4, 1791, and she succumbed on September 6, 1793.)

Therefore, the Pettibone account could be true. The salient point, however, is that belief in "the Demon Vampire" was indeed nothing more than a "strange delusion." Pettibone places the bizarre sacrifice about three years after Rachel's burial, which means the event occurred in early 1793, and Huldah died later that year. Clearly, anti-vampire magic was no cure for consumption.

I attempted to locate Rachel's grave. Isaac Burton and his fourth wife, Dency Raymond (1774–1864), are buried together in the old section of Dellwood Cemetery in Manchester (Holman 1926, 25–28). The graves were relocated there from the old burial ground on the village green, today's courthouse site, where many old, unmarked graves are thought yet to remain (Harwood 2008). Among them may be the lost grave of the beautiful but unfortunate Rachel Harris.

On Woodstock Green

Another story comes from Woodstock, where sources claim a vampire's heart was burned on the public green around 1829. The earliest account appeared in *The Journal of American Folklore* (Curtin 1889, 58–59). The story was later retold in the *Boston Transcript*, followed by an expanded version "Vampirism in Woodstock" in the October 9, 1890, *Vermont Standard* (quoted in Stephens 1970, 71–74). This gave the man's family name as Corwin. (Composite, garbled versions have since appeared [e.g., "Vampire Incidents" 2008].) According to the original source (Curtin 1889, 58):

> The man had died of consumption six months before and his body buried in the ground. A brother of the deceased fell ill soon after, and in a short time it appeared that he too had consumption; when this became known the family determined at once to disinter the body of the dead man and examine his heart. Then they reinterred the body, took the heart to the middle of Woodstock Green, where they kindled a fire under an iron pot, in which they placed the heart, and burned it to ashes.

Unfortunately, not only was the story sixty years old at the time it appeared, but the writer failed to give any source other than an "old lady" in Woodstock who "said she saw the disinterment and the burning with her own eyes." The editor of *The Vermont Standard* added much supplementary material, claiming that the pot of ashes was buried under a seven-ton granite slab and that persons digging at the site a decade later encountered a sulfurous smell and smoke. This reference to the fires of Hell reveal the editor's writing as tongue-in-cheek, even sarcastic, and discredits his other details: the man's name as Corwin and burial in the Cushing Cemetery. Small wonder that no one of that name is buried in that graveyard—as shown by cemetery records (Stillwell and Proctor 1977) and confirmed by a search among the old tombstones by my wife and me (see also Crosier 1986; Wendlong 1990).

Misunderstanding the editor's satire, popular writers have tended either to give too much credence to the story or to debunk or dismiss it altogehter. Possibly the original account did contain a nucleus of truth, an early account of consumption and superstitious belief associated with it.

The Killing Vine

Yet another old case, again involving consumption and associated superstition, has been reinterpreted by moderns as a "vampire incident" ("Vampire" 2008; Rondina 2008, 104). The story, in David L. Mansfield's *The History of the Town of Dummerston* (1884)—itself an account written some ninety years after the events and based on oral tradition—has become somewhat garbled by writers copying writers. Therefore, I tracked down a copy of the original text for study. It relates that Lieutenant Leonard Spaulding died of consumption in 1788, aged fifty-nine, father of eleven children. Mansfield states (1884, 27):

Although the children of Lt. Spaulding, especially the sons, became large, muscular persons, all but one or two died under 40 years of age of consumption, and their sickness was brief.

It is related by those who remember the circumstance; after six or seven of the family had died of consumption, another daughter was taken, it was supposed, with the same disease. It was thought she would die, and much was said in regard to so many of the family's dying of consumption when they all seemed to have the appearance of good health and long life. Among the superstitions of those days, we find it was said that a vine or root of some kind grew from coffin to coffin, of those of one family, who died of consumption, and were buried side by side; and when the growing vine had reached the coffin of the last one buried, another one of the family would die; the only way to destroy the influence or effect, was to break the vine; take up the body of the last one buried and burn the vitals, which would be an effectual remedy: Accordingly, the body of the last one buried was dug up and the vitals taken out and burned, and the daughter, it is affirmed, got well and lived many years. The act, doubtless, raised her mind from a state of despondency to hopefullness [sic].

Now, Spaulding and his wife Margaret (who died in 1827) were buried in separate cemeteries and in unmarked graves. However, I located all but two of the children's graves, including a row of six in the Dummerston Center Cemetery (Figures 1 and 2).

Unfortunately for the quaint legend related by oral tradition, the graves (whether linked by hidden underground vines or not) are not placed consecutively in the order of the family members' deaths. Neither did the last of the six, Josiah, die very close in time to the previous sibling's demise, since more than five-and-a-half years passed since the death of John. Of course, the family may well have been plagued by consumption, and it is possible Josiah's body was disinterred and the vitals burned. In any event, he was indeed followed in death by one of Leonard Spaulding's daughters, as the legend states, since after he died only Olive remained alive. Apparently, she lived on for years, moving with a second husband to Brattleboro (Mansfield 1884, 26)—perhaps this being the secret of her having avoided the contagion!

In New Orleans

In sharp contrast to vampire legends of New England are those of New Orleans. While Louisiana indeed has a folk tradition of werewolves (the Loup-Garous of the Cajuns), the vampire culture there is not folklore but fakelore.

When I investigated various topics in the New Orleans area in 2000

(Nickell 2004, 140–161, 165–175), I found frequent references to vampires. The various nighttime tours focusing on cemeteries, voodoo, and ghosts invariably touted vampires as well, and guides (like mine) regaled tourists with spine-tingling tales of the "undead."

Anne Rice (born Howard Allen O'Brien in 1941) inspired legions of fans with her series of erotic horror novels, beginning with *Interview with the Vampire* (1976). Until she repudiated the genre, returned to her Catholic faith, and moved from New Orleans in 2005, many Rice devotees made pilgrimages to the Big Easy. Some walking tours included Rice's home or the location of the filming of *Interview*. There was even a tour book, *Haunted City: An Unauthorized Guide to the Magical, Magnificent New*

Figure 1. The Spaulding graves of vampire legend in Vermont's Dummerston Center Cemetery.

Figure 2. The author uses chalk to enhance the tombstone of Josiah Spaulding, which is topped with the familiar image of the Angel of Death.

Orleans of Anne Rice (Dickinson 1997).

According to Victor C. Klein, who has compiled two books of New Orleans ghost legends, "Throughout my extensive researches I have never encountered any tangible trace of Vampirism in Louisiana or New Orleans." He adds, "The genesis for such beliefs is directly attributable to the commercial imagination of Ms. Rice and the cerebrotonic endomorphs who, in their mad dash to establish a subjective species of identity and immortality, elevate her works to gospel status" (1999, 106). He also speaks of "the hyperbolic balderdash which spews forth from the black garbed tour guides who are more interested in money and sensationalism than accurate historical research" (1999, 64).

I recall one of the more responsible guides laughingly telling me how a customer once inquired about a particular grave featured in a Rice story and would not be convinced that the site was purely fictional. But I think the evidence shows that that grave is just as authentically vampiric as any real graves in New Orleans, New England, Europe, or elsewhere.

Acknowledgments

My wife, Diana G. Harris, helpfully accompanied me on my trip to Vermont. Timothy Binga, director of CFI Libraries, provided much research assistance, and I am grateful to Paul Loynes for typesetting and indeed the entire *Skeptical Inquirer* staff for help at all levels.

I am especially grateful to the following gracious Vermont people and institutions for their crucial assistance: in Woodstock, the staff of the Norman Williams Public Library, including reference-desk attendant John Donaldson, and the staff of the Woodstock Inn and Resort (for free coffee and tea!); in Dummerston, Town Clerk Pam McFadden and historian Paul Normandeau; and in Manchester, the staff of the Mark Skinner Library, Assistant Town Clerk Bear Scovil, Dellwood Cemetery caretaker Kurt Baccei, and, especially, curator of the Manchester Historical Society, Dr. Judy Harwood.

References

Citro, Joseph A. 1994. *Green Mountain Ghosts, Ghouls and Unsolved Mysteries*. Boston: Houghton Mifflin.

Crosier, Barney. 1986. Vermont's vampire heart. *Rutland Herald*, October 26.

Curtin, Jeremiah. 1889. European folk-lore in the United States. *Journal of American Folklore*. 2:4 (March), 56–59.

Dickinson, Joy. 1997. *Haunted City: An Unauthorized Guide to the Magical, Magnificent New Orleans of Anne Rice*. Secaucus, N.J.: Citadel Press.

"Exhumed the Bodies . . . ." 1892. *Provincetown Journal*, March 19 (reprinted in Rondina 2008, 86–87).

Harwood, Judy. 2008. Personal communication, May 21, July 9.

Holman, Winifred Lovering. 1926. *Descendants of Josiah Burton of Manchester*, Vt. Concord, N.H.: The Rumford Press.

Klein, Victor C. 1999. *New Orleans Ghosts II*. Metairie, La.: Lycanthrope Press.

Mansfield, David L. 1884. *The History of the Town of Dummerston*. Ludlow, Vt.: Published by Miss A.M. Hemenway.

Nickell, Joe. 2004. *The Mystery Chronicles: More Real-Life X-Files*. Lexington, Ky.: University Press of Kentucky.

Proceedings of the Vermont Historical Society. 1930. New series, vol. 1, no. 4.

Ramsland, Katherine. 2002. *The Science of Vampires*. New York: Berkley Boulevard Books.

Rice, Anne. 1976. *Interview with the Vampire*, New York: Alfred A. Knopf.

Rondina, Christopher. 2008. *Vampires of New England*. N.p.: On the Cape Publications.

Stoker, Bram. 1897. *Dracula*. Reprinted, New York: Barnes & Noble, 2003.

Stillwell, Dorothy, and Dorothy L. Proctor. 1977. Cushing cemetery file; typescript at Norman Williams Public Library, Woodstock, Vermont.

Vampire incidents in New England. 2008. Available online at www.foodforthe dead.com/map.swf; accessed May 9.

"The Vampire Theory." 1892. *Providence Journal*, March 21; reprinted in Rondina 2008, 89–96.

Wendling, Kathy. 1990. Woodstock's vampire: The heart of the legend. *Vermont Standard*, October 25.

Peru's Ancient Mysteries

Peru, like all the Americas, was relatively recently settled (an occurrence made possible by the last Ice Age, which allowed humans to cross the now-inundated Bering Land Bridge between present-day Russia and Alaska). A succession of native cultures flourished in various regions and eventually metamorphosed into the Inca Empire. This began in the Andean highlands circa 1200 C.E. and—by the Spanish Conquest of the 1530s—ranged from Ecuador south to Chile.

Ancient mysteries abound in Peru, several of which I was able to look into prior to speaking at the Second Ibero-American Conference on Critical Thinking held in Lima, August 3–5, 2006. Here, I report on the remarkable Nasca Lines, the oracle at the stepped-pyramid complex of Pachacamac, and the curiously fanciful Ica stones.

Nasca Lines

It had taken me years to arrive in Nasca (formerly "Nazca"), a dusty town in the San José desert made famous by its nearby enigmatic geoglyphs. These giant ground drawings—consisting of straight lines, great trapezoids, and stylized birds and other figures—were made by the pre-Incan Nasca culture that flourished in the area from 200 B.C.E. to about 600 C.E. Their graves and the ruins of their settlements lie near the drawings, and Nasca pottery shards are intermingled with the desert gravel.

The figures are so large they can only be properly viewed from the air (Figure 1). Thus they have prompted crank notions that they were created by "ancient astronauts." That idea was hyped by the ridiculous—though worldwide-best-selling—*Chariots of the Gods?* written by Erich von Däniken (1970). A somewhat less absurd concept was still

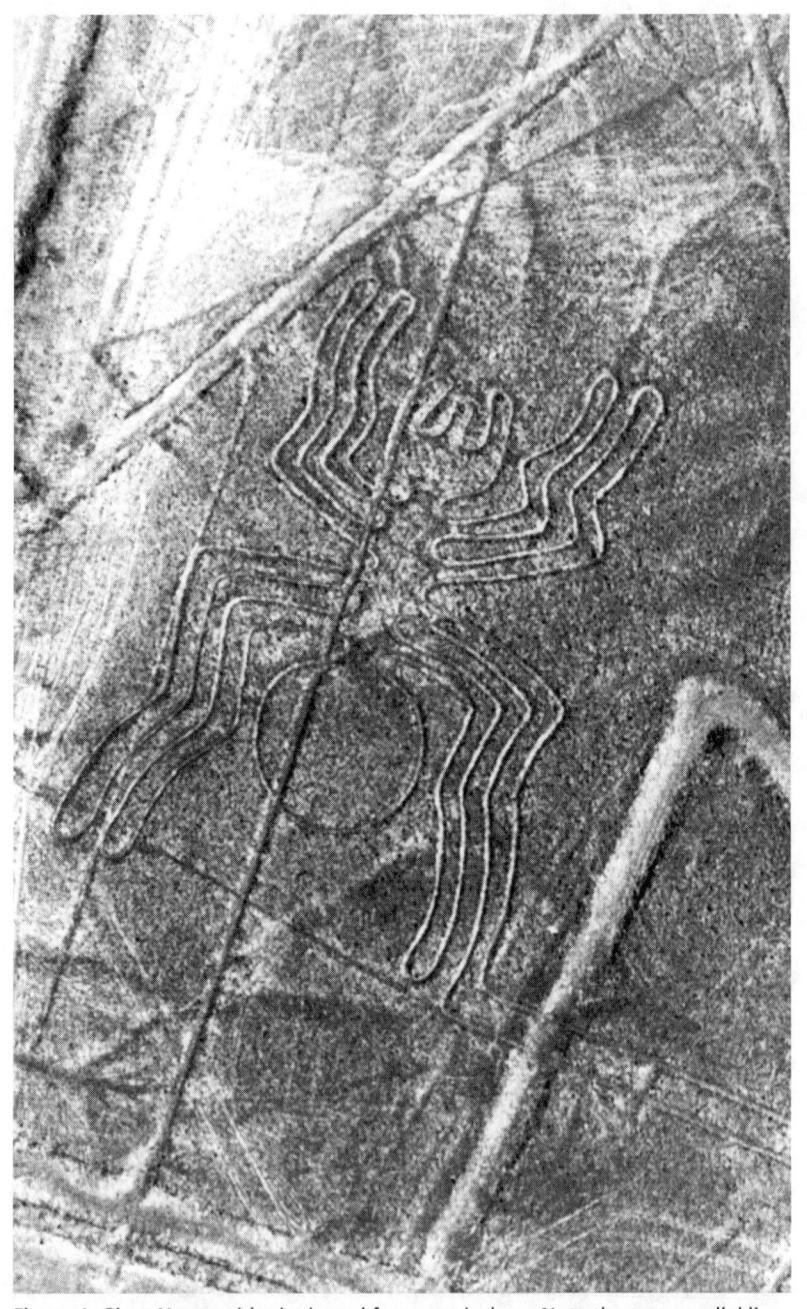

Figure 1. Giant Nasca spider is viewed from an airplane. Note the two parallel lines extending from the lower right leg. (Overflight photo by Benjamin Radford)

full of hot air: it held that the ancient Nascas had invented ballooning and made ceremonial flights over the *pampas* (Woodman 1977).

In my first article for the *Skeptical Inquirer*, I reported on my experimental re-creation in 1982 of one of the largest figures, the giant "condor" that measures some 440 feet from beak to tail. For a giant sketch pad, I used a landfill area near my childhood hometown, utilizing only a pair of crossed sticks (for sighting) and two knotted lengths of cord (for measuring). I discredited the idea that the Nascas used either the grid method of enlargement or a traverse surveying technique. Instead, I enlarged a small drawing by establishing first a center line, then measuring down it until directly opposite a desired point (for example, a wing tip), and again measuring from there to the point itself. We repeated the process on the ground, substituting *larger* units and finally connecting the points to complete the drawing (Nickell 1983). (My father handled most of the logistics, and my cousin Sid Haney the bulk of the construction work from our crew of six.) Whereas the Nasca Lines are made by removing the dark desert gravel and thus exposing the lighter earth, we marked our figure with white lime, in the way one marks a playing field.

We then flew over the area at about a thousand feet, the pilot banking the plane so another cousin, John May, could lean out and photograph our condor straight-on, while I held onto his belt as a safety measure. Because, as *Scientific American* ("Big" 1983) noted, our drawing was "remarkable in its exactness" to the original, I concluded that the Nasca probably used an even simpler version of this technique, with a significant amount of work being done freehand (Nickell 1983).

Twenty-four years later, in 2006, I was asked to come out of retirement and make another, this time for National Geographic Television's series *Is It Real?* The producers had chosen the giant spider, and, with only a couple of helpers, I drew it handily in one day, while they filmed the process from a cherry picker (Figure 2).

Not long afterward—and very belatedly—I was able to fly over the original Nasca geoglyphs, accompanied by *Skeptical Inquirer* then managing editor Benjamin Radford. We traveled by bus from Lima and commissioned one of the small, light airplanes that make regular flights over the area. We ignored a travel-guide warning to "avoid breakfast before flying" (Wehner and Gaudio 2004, 234), hoped the one-eyed man who picked us up at our hotel was not our pilot, and bravely faced evidence that our actual pilot had tanked up on *pisco* (white-grape brandy) be-

Figure 2. Author stands in his recreation of Nasca spider, made on a California ranch for National Geographic Television. (Photo by Joe Nickell)

fore the flight. Even though during steep turns the pilot would turn around to chat with me in the back seat, there were no disasters.

The July 31 flight fulfilled one of my longstanding dreams, as we flew not only over the condor and spider—who now were like old friends to me—but also the monkey, whale, heron, and many other figures. (Later, I would myself celebrate with pisco—the pisco sour being Peru's national drink. I even learned to make the cocktail from our Lima hotel bartender, amusingly a Peter Lorre look-alike.)

Before leaving Nasca, we were also able to observe a few geoglyphs from an observation tower, walk a segment of one long line (otherwise walking on the markings is prohibited), and visit the Casa-Museo Maria Reiche. Named for the German mathematician who devoted her life to studying and preserving the lines, this is where she lived until her death in 1998 at age ninety-five. (When she died, Nasca town officials proclaimed a day of mourning, and German and Peruvian flags were lowered to half-staff. The Peruvian president called it "a really painful and sad loss for Peruvian archaeology." Just how painful a loss was underscored two months after Reiche's death, when American tourists drove their van across the arid plain, scarring the geoglyphs with tire tracks that, according to the Associated Press, "will remain for centuries" [Nickell 1998].)

Featured at the hacienda-turned-museum were Maria Reiche's simple room, her Nasca measuring and drawing instruments, aerial photos of the geoglyphs, and other related items. Outside were her VW van and—in a beautiful garden lined with multicolored bougainvilleas—her grave.

Despite Maria Reiche's selfless work, many mysteries remain, notably that of why the geoglyphs were made. In his admirable book, *Nasca: Eighth Wonder of the World?*, anthropologist and astronomy professor Anthony Aveni reported the results of extensive studies of the Nasca lines. The studies fail to substantiate any astronomical significance, but the lines so correlate with geographic features as to suggest that they were used as mystical walking paths—"labyrinths"—during irrigation rituals (Aveni 2000, 212–222).

Inspired by this possibility, I took a new look at the drawings, observing several strongly suggestive elements. Not only do the figures look like paths (being cleared of gravel) and often have decidedly *winding* elements (e.g., the monkey's spiral tail and a bird's sinuous neck), but there are two features that offer further evidence of their purpose. First, unlike ordinary Nasca depictions (as on pottery), the figures are drawn with a continuous line. Second, they typically have an extraneous pair of lines (such as extend from the spider's lower right leg [again see Figure 1]). Significantly, *if one walks into one of these lines, he or she is led to traverse the entire figure and exit from the other line*—seeming to confirm that the geoglyphs were indeed ceremonial paths (Nickell 2004).

This recognition takes us a step further in attempting to understand the legacy of the still mysterious Nasca people.

Oracle at Pachacamac

In the Lurín Valley, about thirty kilometers south of Lima, stands the sacred citadel of Pachacamac. An extensive archeological site, it is a complex of adobe-brick buildings and pyramids, spanning various ancient cultures. Pachacamac was the dominant pilgrimage center on Peru's central coast and "home to the most feared, and respected, oracle in the Andes" (Wehner and Gaudio 2004, 283).

On August 2, I commissioned a personal tour of the citadel, enlisting a driver and professional guide. Like countless pilgrims of the Wari-Ishmay and later Inca cultures, I walked the sandy streets, climbed the stepped pyramids, and gazed from the heights of Pachacamac (Figure 3). Albeit for different reasons, I too was in quest of the mysterious oracle.

At this Andean citadel, the god Pachacamac—whose name in the

Figure 3. A Peruvian guide helps identify one of the stepped pyramids at Pachacamac. (Photo by Joe Nickell)

Incan language, Quechua, means "Lord of the World"—reigned supreme. According to native mythology, Pachacamac, the Creator, took as his wife Urpiwachak, who was goddess of fish and birds. (A pyramid temple with her name stands in the northwest part of the city near a now-dry lagoon.) Among Pachacamac's countless roles were protector of food, controller of earthquakes, and healer of diseases (*Pachakamaq* n.d., 35).

Few details are known about the oracle, but one naturally thinks of Ancient Greece's Oracle of Delphi. There, worshipers believed, the Pythian priestesses channeled the god Apollo after inhaling the fumes and drinking the waters of a bubbling spring that ran beneath the temple. According to Owen S. Rachleff, in his *The Occult Conceit* (1971, 137):

> It is quite obvious that the Oracle was simply intoxicated by some form of narcotic that had been naturally or artificially dissolved in the waters of the spring. The pertinent factor, however, especially as it concerns modern precognition, is the subsequent interpretation given her ravings by the Delphic priests. Most often these interpretations were offerings of good advice on matters of war, marriage, finance, and the like. But when the priests were asked for specific predictions—the bane of all seers—they cloaked their reports in clever ambiguities that, coupled with the ambiguous condition of human life, served as an effective ploy. Thus the name of a king or prince babbled by the Oracle might mean

prosperity or calamity for the kingdom or personal harm (or fortune) for the king. If the king was later involved in a crisis, either good or bad—as kings or rulers are wont to be—the priests could take credit for a significant prophecy; something, they would say, was in the air concerning their king.

The wooden idol of Pachacamac (now in the on-site museum but "probably a replica" [Wehner and Gaudio 2004, 283]) was carved with various figures and symbols representing "a cosmic vision of the Andean world" of the twelfth century (*Pachakamaq* n.d., 11). At the top of the long, cylindrical idol stands, Janus-like, a two-faced figure, apparently representing Pachacamac's oracular ability. This is evident in the deity's being able to see in opposite directions and so, symbolically, to divine the past and future. According to chroniclers, copies of the idol were placed in several different parts of the city (*Pachakamaq* n.d., 11).

As we now know, the oracle met its match in the two-facedness of Francisco Pizarro (ca. 1471–1541). Searching for gold and other riches, Pizarro spent nearly two years traveling across South America's mountains and deserts to locate the heart of the great Inca Empire. The Inca king Atahualpa had received assurance from the oracle at Pachacamac that he would be victorious against the bearded white men who ventured into his land. He expected to sacrifice most to the sun god, keeping only a few as castrated servants, while capturing and breeding the Spaniards' remarkable horses.

Pizarro had ideas of his own. He sent a friendly invitation to Atahualpa to join him at Cajamarca, the Incan gold-production center, in mid-November 1523. Arriving early, Pizarro stationed his 170 men in three empty warehouses that flanked the main square. While Atahualpa arrived with 5,000 warriors, he was so confident of supremacy that they were ceremonially dressed and only lightly armed. The king was ostentatiously borne on a litter by eighty Inca officials.

Under Pizarro's direction, a Dominican friar approached Atahualpa and explained that he had come to spread the Catholic faith, offering the king a little breviary (a book of instructions for the recitation of Catholic daily services). Outraged at this presumption, Atahualpa flung the book to the ground, whereupon the conquistadors launched a surprise attack with trumpets blaring, cannon blazing, and armored men on horseback charging with swords and lances. The Incans panicked and fled but were slaughtered in great numbers while many others were suffocated in the crush of bodies.

Captured and imprisoned, Atahualpa bitterly complained of the

Pachacamac oracle's false prediction that he would prevail over the Spaniards. He soon offered the Spaniards a king's ransom: in return for his freedom, he would fill a big room (almost 88 cubic meters) with gold and two more with silver. Pizarro agreed, and, as the sacred and other priceless items arrived, he had nine furnaces run continuously to convert them into bars—an estimated 13,420 pounds of 22-karat gold and 26,000 of good-quality silver.

Despite the ransom, a majority of the Spanish officers decided to execute Atahualpa anyway, fearing he was plotting against them. The king agreed to a last-minute baptism—apparently to avoid an infidel's fate of being burned at the stake—and was hanged (Wehner and Gaudio 2004, 283, 460). The oracle of Pachacamac had failed not only to see the ruler's defeat, but his death as well.

Now Pizarro was drawn to the citadel by Atahualpa's accounts of golden treasures there. He and a troop of his soldiers made a three-week ride to the site. Shoving the Incan priests aside, the conquistador strode to the top of the stepped pyramid where he found a building fashioned of cane and mud, its door adorned with gemstones. In its dark interior he found the roughly carved effigy of Pachacamac. As he wrote, "Seeing the filth and mockery of the idol, we went out to ask why they thought highly of something so dirty and ugly" (qtd. in Wehner and Gaudio 2004, 283).

Pizarro should have looked critically as his own situation. Living by the sword and failing to follow many of the commandments of his own professed faith, he quarreled with his officers over power, had one executed, and was in turn assassinated by that man's followers—a sordid episode in the sordid history of religious conquest.

Ica Stones

On the Pan American highway between Lima and Nasca lies Ica, a town in the desert of the same name that bears one of the world's greatest deposits of marine fossils. On the Plaza de Armas in Ica is found the Museo Cabrera, which features thousands of enigmatic stones. They are covered with engraved drawings purportedly made by some astonishingly sophisticated ancient civilization (see Figure 4).

Bearing depictions of ancient men using telescopes, performing heart surgery and brain transplants, piloting flying machines, hunting dinosaurs, riding on the backs of pterodactyls, and other fantastic scenes, the rocks began to appear in 1966. At that time, a Peruvian physician, Javier Cabrera Darques, was given a carved rock as a birth-

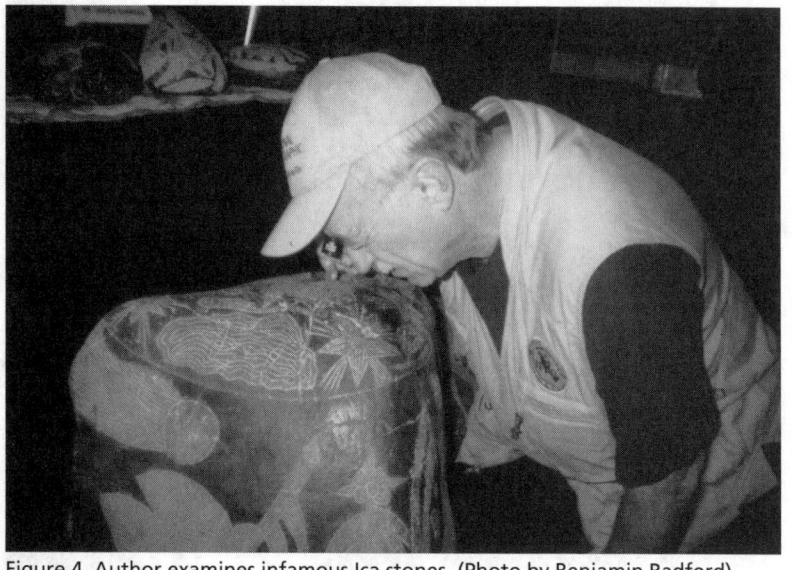

Figure 4. Author examines infamous Ica stones. (Photo by Benjamin Radford)

day gift. It depicted an extinct fish, but it was Cabrera who was hooked: he learned that locals could supply him with more fabulous stones and he began to purchase them.

Cabrera was told that the engraved stones were discovered in a cave, but its location was never revealed. Nevertheless, he came to believe the artifacts were made by an advanced race. Cabrera abandoned his Lima medical practice, created in Ica a Museo de Piedras Grabadas ("Museum of Engraved Stones")—now the Museo Cabrera—and proceeded to stock it with as many as 15,000 stones before his death in 2002 (Polidoro 2002; Wehner and Gaudio 2004, 244; Carroll 2004, 43–44). Cabrera insisted that the rocks were volcanic andesite that, being too hard to carve with simple stone tools, indicated the drawings were made by an extraterrestrial race he called *Gliptolithic Man* (Ica stones 2006).

As it happens, a peasant named Basilio Uschuya who had been "discovering" Ica stones was arrested by Peruvian authorities following a 1996 BBC documentary on the carvings. Charged with selling archeological treasures, he admitted that the carvings were fakes that he and his wife had produced with a dentist's drill and antiqued by baking the stones in dung (Ica stones 2006).

Nevertheless, the stones are still heralded by "ancient-astronaut" advocates (*à la* Von Däniken), fundamentalist creationists (who believe that man and dinosaurs coexisted), and other fringe types, including the "mytho-historians" (who hold that ancient mythologies should be taken literally) (Carroll 2002).

The stones' defenders include "psychic" Sylvia Browne (2005, 116) whose spirit guide Francine tells her the stones "were indeed a record left behind by extraterrestrials who inhabited the area millions of years ago." Browne (2005, 114) insists, "German laboratories have authenticated that the carvings on the stones are indeed very ancient" and bear a "patina of oxidation over them" (2005, 114).

Benjamin Radford and I stopped in Ica on our way to Nasca. On Sunday, July 30, the Museo Cabrera being closed, we had our hotel manager call and offer a cash payment for a special showing. We were met at the museum by Emma Hernandez, who took us inside the stone-filled office and two storerooms and generously allowed us to photograph and inspect the vast collection of Ica stones. Sitting at Cabrera's desk, I used a 10× Bausch & Lomb illuminated loupe to examine the engraved lines.

Subsequently, we were directed to a store across the plaza where we were told we might be able to purchase Ica stones. The proprietor brought out several from under a counter for us to view, and I purchased one depicting a man riding a dinosaur that did not have the added coloration and allowed me to see the stone's original dark patina of age. (I was later able to examine this stone with a stereomicroscope and make some simple tests.) We were also able, on two occasions, to watch Ica-type stone sellers easily and quickly produce Nasca imagery with a simple engraving tool.

The Ica stones I examined were not physically remarkable. They are simply weathered stones that do have a patina of what is called "desert varnish," and this is merely incised to produce the drawings. By their being engraved rather than carved, the hardness of the rock itself is not an issue, despite the claims of some. Cabrera's stones have been given a coating of boot polish—as the museum readily acknowledges—applied to enhance the lines. While this obscures the natural oxidized coating, the salient point is that the patina is completely absent from the inscribed lines—revealing that the engravings are of relatively recent vintage.

Acknowledgments

In addition to individuals already mentioned, I am grateful to those who made possible the second Ibero-American Conference on Critical Thinking. These include—of course—Paul Kurtz, Barry Karr, and dedicated CFI staffers. I also greatly appreciate the efforts of Manuel A. Paz y Miño of Peru for his assistance in many ways.

References

Aveni, Anthony F. 2000. *Nasca: Eighth Wonder of the World?* London: British Museum Press.

The big picture. 1983. *Scientific American* 248(6) (June): 84.

Browne, Sylvia. 2005. *Secrets & Mysteries of the World.* Carlsbad, California: Hay House.

Carroll, Robert Todd. 2002. The Ica stones in: *The Skeptic's Dictionary.* Available at http://skepdic.com/icastones.html.

———. 2004. Pranks, frauds and hoaxes from around the world. *Skeptical Inquirer* 28(4) (July/August): 41–46.

Ica stones. 2006. Wikipedia entry. Available at http://en.wikipedia.org/w/index.php?title=Ica_stones&printable=yes; accessed June 29.

Nickell, Joe. 1983. The Nazca drawings revisited: Creation of a full-sized duplicate. *Skeptical Inquirer* 7(3) (Spring): 36–44.

———. 1998. Maria Reiche, Nazca lines' guardian, dies. *Skeptical Inquirer* 22(6) (November/December): 16.

———. 2004. Nasca: "laberintos en el desierto." *Pensar* 1(3) (July–September): 17–20.

Pachakamaq: Ciudad sagrada. N.d. An archaeological guide sold on site. N.p.: n.p.

Polidoro, Massimo. 2002. Ica stones: Yabba-Dabba-Do! *Skeptical Inquirer* 26(5) (September/October): 24–25.

Rachleff, Owen St. 1971. *The Occult Conceit: A New Look at Astrology, Witchcraft & Sorcery.* Chicago: Cowles.

Von Däniken, Erich. 1970. *Chariots of the Gods?* New York: G.P. Putnam.

Wehner, Ross, and Renée Del Gaudio. 2004. *Moon Handbooks Peru.* Emeryville, Calif.: Avalon Travel Publishing.

Woodman, Jim. 1977. *Nazca: Journey to the Sun.* New York: Pocket Books.

John Edward:
Spirit Huckster

"Psychic medium" John Edward is reemerging from relative obscurity after his popular television show, *Crossing Over with John Edward*, ended in 2004. He appears on another cable show, gives tours, has a website (Infinitequest.com), and generally makes his living claiming to communicate with those who have "crossed over."

I was invited by Central New York Skeptics to join them in Syracuse, New York, for an evening with Edward. (It was held at Mulroy Civic Center on Sunday, October 11, 2009. I was accompanied by CNY Skeptics President Lisa Goodlin, David Harding, and Brian Madigan, all of whom afterward shared insightful observations on what we had witnessed.) The glib Edward—real name John Edward McGee, Jr.—held forth for more than two hours. He began with a joke to the effect that although he is psychic, he nevertheless needed a GPS to get to the site.

The highly credulous, adoring crowd seemed to find every gag hilarious, every platitude profound, and every lucky guess or shrewd deduction proof of communication with the dead.

Old 'Spirits' in New Bottles

Edward is part of the new breed of spiritualists (like Sylvia Browne and James Van Praagh) who avoid the risky *physical* mediumship of yore. During the heyday of Spiritualism, magicians such as Houdini and Maskelyne used to catch mediums at their dark-room séance deceptions, such as slate writing, floating spirit trumpets, and full-bodied "materializations." The investigators gave public demonstrations of the trickery. "Do Spirits Return?" a Houdini poster asked. "Houdini says No—and Proves It" (Gibson 1977, 157).

The new "psychic mediums" opt instead for the simpler, safer *mental* mediumship, the supposed production of messages from the Great Beyond. This itself is nothing new, but now instead of the flowery language supposedly channeled from talkative Victorians, we get fragmented bits of data from spirits seeming to have diminished memories and limited speech: "I feel like there's a J- or G-sounding name attached to this" is a typical Edward offering (Nickell 2001).

Styles change even in supposedly talking with the dead. Today's mediums employ the old fortuneteller's technique of "cold reading"—so named because the sensitive has no advance information about the sitter. He artfully fishes for information from the person, often asking a question which, if the answer is yes, will be treated as a "hit" but otherwise will become only part of the lead-up to a statement.

Not surprisingly, Edward has a background in fortunetelling. His mother, he acknowledges, was a "psychic junkie" who threw fortunetelling "house parties." Advised by one visiting clairvoyant that he had "wonderful psychic abilities," Edward began doing card readings for family and friends as a teenager. He progressed to giving readings at so-called psychic fairs. There he soon learned that names and other "validating information" could sometimes be better fitted to the dead than the living. Edward eventually changed his billing from "psychic" to "psychic medium" (Edward 1999), setting him on the road to financial success.

The Group Approach

Edward's audiences typically find him accurate and convincing. However, a study I made of one television transcript[1] revealed he was actually wrong about as often as not (Nickell 1998). In Syracuse, for example, no one seemed to relate to a cat named Smokey. Nevertheless, in such cases Edward can still toss out something he "sees" or "feels," and he may get lucky. Besides, the onus is on his listeners to somehow match his offerings to their lives, and if one person can't oblige, someone else will give it a try. Thus, when no one seemed to be "going to Thailand," Edward doubled his options, suggesting the trip was for adoption. Finally, one woman shouted out that she had adopted a child from Korea. When no one had experienced an Edward-visualized tattoo removal, a young lady helpfully supplied her adventure of an excised mole. Edward then looked for validation of an imagined spirit named Lily: She soon morphed into a cat of that name, still living!

Edward sometimes joked his way out of a dilemma. For instance, when one woman's late husband had not had the envisioned "foot surgery," Edward quipped, "Do you have any other husbands?"

Joking aside, this group approach has been a boon to modern mediums. On occasion, when multiple sitters acknowledge a particular offering, the medium can simply narrow the choice to a single person and then build on that success—a technique definitely employed by John Edward (Ballard 2001).

Getting Burned with 'Hot' Reading

According to respected journalists, episodes of *Crossing Over* were edited to make Edward appear more accurate than he was (Ballard 2001), even to the point of apparently splicing in clips of one sitter nodding yes "after statements with which he remembers disagreeing" (Jaroff 2001).

Rarely, when the opportunity presents itself, Edward may turn from "cold reading" to the much more accurate "hot reading." Although I have no evidence of him using that technique in Syracuse, he was caught cheating with it on a *Dateline NBC* episode for which I was both a behind-the-scenes advisor and an on-camera interviewee. Edward was exposed passing off knowledge he had gained from a *Dateline* cameraman during a shoot hours earlier as otherworldly revelation during a reading session. He feigned surprise that his alleged spirit gleanings applied to the cameraman. As *Dateline*'s John Hockenberry subsequently told an evasive Edward, "So that's not some energy coming through, that's something you knew going in" (Nickell 2001).

In his book, *Crossing Over*, Edward disparaged Hockenberry who, he said, "came down on the side of the professional skeptic they used as my foil . . . Joe Nickell" (2001, 243). Edward also referred to Hockenberry's "big Gotcha! moment." That's right, John, we gotcha! You were caught cheating. And your claimed psychic powers didn't even let you see it coming.

Fast Talker

In his stand-up act, Edward keeps things going at such a pace that there is little time to critically analyze what is occurring. The average person is not much better equipped to avoid being fooled by John Edward's sleight-of-tongue tricks than the artful illusions of a stage magician. Careful analysis of a recorded session by one knowledgeable of the techniques employed will prove more effective than the testimonials of someone fooled by the deceptions.

And so Edward's Syracuse audience regarded their belief in other-worldly communication as fully vindicated. There appeared to be only about four skeptics in the audience. Ironically, Edward seemed not to know they were there—even though one has been a particular thorn in his side. Couldn't he feel all those bad vibes coming from an area of the orchestra?

Acknowledgments

In addition to those mentioned in the text, I am also grateful to Barry Karr, CSI executive director, for providing finances for my trip to Syracuse and to Timothy Binga, Center for Inquiry Libraries director, for research assistance.

Note

1. This was the June 19, 1998, *Larry King Live* show on CNN.

References

Ballard, Chris. 2001. Oprah of the other side. *The New York Times Magazine*, July 29, 38–41.
Edward, John. 1999. *One Last Time*. New York: Berkeley Books.
———. 2001. *Crossing Over: The Stories Behind the Stories*. San Diego, CA: Jodere Group.
Gibson, Walter B. 1977. *The Original Houdini Scrapbook*. New York: Corwin/Sterling.
Jaroff, Leon. 2001. Talking to the dead. *Time*, March 5, 52.
Nickell, Joe. 1998. Investigating spirit communications. *Skeptical Briefs* 8:3 (September), 5–6.
———. 2001. John Edward: Hustling the bereaved. *Skeptical Inquirer* 25:6 (November/December), 19–22.

The Secrets of Oak Island

It has been the focus of "the world's longest and most expensive treasure hunt" and "one of the world's deepest and most costly archaeological digs" (O'Connor 1988, 1, 4), as well as being "Canada's best-known mystery" (Colombo 1988, 33) and indeed one of "the great mysteries of the world." It may even "represent an ancient artifact created by a past civilization of advanced capability" (Crooker 1978, 7, 190). The subject of these superlatives is a mysterious shaft on Oak Island in Nova Scotia's Mahone Bay. For some two centuries, greed, folly, and even death have attended the supposed "Money Pit" enigma.

The Saga

Briefly, the story is that in 1795 a young man named Daniel McInnis (or McGinnis) was roaming Oak Island when he came upon a shallow depression in the ground. Above it, hanging from the limb of a large oak was an old tackle block. McInnis returned the next day with two friends who—steeped in the local lore of pirates and treasure troves—set to work to excavate the site. They soon uncovered a layer of flagstones and, ten feet farther, a tier of rotten oak logs. They proceeded another fifteen feet into what they were sure was a man-made shaft but, tired from their efforts, they decided to cease work until they could obtain assistance. However, between the skepticism and superstition of the people who lived on the mainland, they were unsuccessful.

The imagined cache continued to lie dormant until early in the next century, when the trio joined with a businessman named Simeon Lynds from the town of Onslow to form a treasure-hunting consortium called the Onslow Company. Beginning work about 1803 or 1804 (one source says 1810), they found oak platforms "at exact intervals of ten feet"

(O'Connor 1978, 10), along with layers of clay, charcoal, and a fibrous material identified as coconut husks. Then, at ninety feet (or eighty feet, according to one alleged participant) they supposedly found a flat stone bearing an indecipherable inscription (see Figure 1). Soon after, probing with a crowbar, they struck something hard—possibly a wooden chest!—but discontinued for the evening. Alas, the next morning the shaft was found flooded with sixty feet of water. Attempting to bail out the pit with buckets, they found the water level remained the same, and they were forced to discontinue the search. The following year, the men attempted to bypass the water by means of a parallel shaft from which they hoped to tunnel to the supposed treasure. But this shaft suffered the same fate, and the Onslow Company's expedition ended (O'Connor 1978, 9–16; Crooker 1993, 14; Harris 1958, 12–22).

Again the supposed cache lay dormant until in 1849 another group, the Truro Company, reexcavated the original shaft. Encountering water, the workers then set up a platform in the pit and used a hand-operated auger to drill and remove cores of material. They found clay, bits of

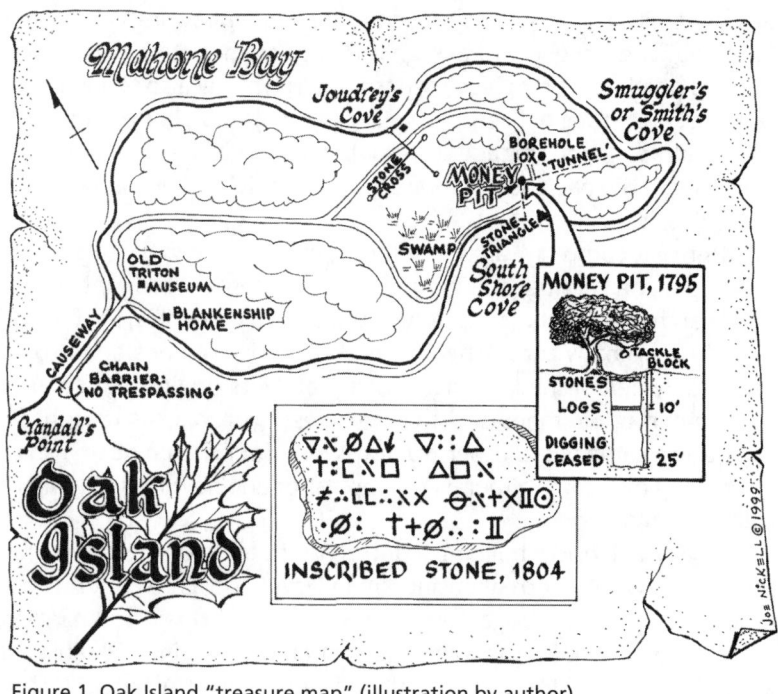

Figure 1. Oak Island "treasure map" (illustration by author).

wood, and three links of gold chain—supposed evidence of buried treasure. The Truro Company sank additional nearby shafts, but these, too, were inundated with water, and work ceased in the fall of 1850. Other operations continued from 1858 to 1862, during which time a workman was scalded to death by a ruptured boiler (O'Connor 1988, 17–31).

The Oak Island Association followed and attempted to intersect the "tunnel" that presumably fed water to the pit. When that 120-foot shaft missed, another was sunk and, reportedly, a three-by-four-foot tunnel was extended about eighteen feet to the "Money Pit" (as it was then known). However, water began coming in again. A massive bailing operation was then set up when suddenly there was a loud crash as the Money Pit collapsed. It was later theorized that the imagined chests had fallen into a deep void and that the pit may have been booby-trapped to protect the treasure (O'Connor 1988, 29). The Association's work was followed in 1866 by the Oak Island Eldorado Company but without significant results (Harris 1958, 203).

Decades elapsed and in 1897 the Oak Island Treasure Company (incorporated four years earlier) apparently located the long-sought "pirate tunnel" that led from Smith's Cove to the Money Pit. They drilled and dynamited to close off the tunnel. Subsequent borings were highlighted by the discovery of a fragment of parchment upon which was penned portions of two letters (possibly "ri"). They also found traces of a chalk-like stone or "cement" (Harris 1958, 91–98). In this same year Oak Island's second tragedy struck when a worker was being hoisted from one of the pits and the rope slipped from its pulley, plunging him to his death.

After that company ran out of funds, most of the moveable assets were sold at a sheriff's sale in 1900. The new century brought continued searches, with the digging of innumerable drill holes, shafts, and tunnels—so many that "The entire Money Pit area has been topographically demolished, changing completely its original appearance and rendering old maps and charts useless" (Crooker 1978, 190). In 1965 there came yet another tragedy when four men died in a shaft after being overcome either by swamp gas or engine fumes (O'Connor 1988, 143–145).

In 1966 a Florida building contractor named Dan Blankenship teamed up with Montréal businessman David Tobias to continue the quest. The partners began an extensive drilling operation, sinking some sixty bore-holes the following year alone, and, in 1968, enlisted a number of investors in what they named Triton Alliance. Unfortunately, mechanical problems, land disputes, the Stock Market crash of 1987, and other troubles, including the eventual falling out of the two partners, stopped their projected $10 million "big dig" (Randle 1995). Once open to tourists, the site sank into neglect.

Over the years the fabled treasure has been the target of dowsers, automatic writers, clairvoyants, channelers, tarot-card readers, dream interpreters, psychic archaeologists, and assorted other visionaries and soothsayers, as well as crank inventors of devices like a "Mineral Wave Ray" and an airplane-borne "treasure smelling" machine—not one having been successful (Preston 1988, 62; O'Connor 1988, 121–136; Finnan 1997, 166–170).

An Investigative Approach

The more elusive the treasure has proved, the more speculation it has engendered. Given the "immense amount of labor" presumably required to construct the pit and the accompanying "flooding tunnel" that served as a "booby trap," presumption of a pirates' hoard has begun to be supplanted by such imagined prizes as the French crown jewels, Shakespeare's manuscripts, the "lost treasure" of the Knights Templar, even the Holy Grail and the imagined secrets of the "lost continent" of Atlantis (Sora 1999, 7–38, 101; Crooker 1978, 153).

But is there a treasure at the bottom of the "Money Pit"? My research into the mystery of Oak Island dates back many years, and I opened a file on the case in 1982. However, except for periodic updates, I put it on hold, largely because the solution seemed to lie in the same direction as those of some other mysteries (Nickell 1980; 1982a; 1982b). However, when asked to address a forensic conference in nearby New Brunswick, I resolved to place Oak Island on my itinerary (Nickell 2000).

In planning my trip I attempted to contact Triton's David Tobias, who did not, however, return my call, but I did reach Jim Harvey at the Oak Island Inn and Marina on the nearby mainland. Harvey, a retired Royal Canadian Mounted Police officer and licensed private investigator, is in charge of security for Oak Island, and he was adamant that it is no longer open to visitors. Making not-so-veiled references to the legendary temper of Dan Blankenship, the other Triton partner who still lives on the island, Harvey suggested it would not be safe for me to trespass on the island, although he offered for hire his cabin cruiser for a guided circumnavigation.

Harvey may have had in mind an incident of many years ago, involving an altercation between Blankenship and another island resident, Frederick Nolan. According to one source: "One day Blankenship had approached with a rifle in hand and an ugly situation had begun to develop. Eventually the police were called in to calm everybody down and confiscate the gun" (Finnan 1997, 93).

So it was with some trepidation that—on the afternoon of July 1, 1991, after arriving at the village of Western Shore and checking in at the Oak Island Inn—I drove to the causeway leading to Oak Island. This land bridge connecting the island to the mainland was constructed in 1965 so that a great excavating machine could be transported to the "treasure" area. Today it is chained off and marked "Private/No Hunting or Trespassing/Danger."

A local fisherman responded to my proposal to walk over and talk to Mr. Blankenship: "He won't shoot you, but he will probably turn you back." In fact, although Blankenship was at first stand-offish, having read a Canadian Press article about the "professional skeptic" who was heading to Oak Island (see Nickell 2000), I soon mollified him, and he graciously invited me to his home. I was there until nearly 11 PM, being shown artifacts, photos, papers, and a video made by a camera lowered into a borehole—the fruits of almost thirty-five years of treasure hunting that had earned Blankenship the title of "Oak Island's most obsessive searcher" (O'Connor 1988, 145). The video reveals the interior of a "tunnel," graced with an apparent upright timber and what some imagine to be "chests," a "scoop," and other supposed artifacts. Blankenship (1999) told me he had located the site of the borehole by dowsing. The next day Jim Harvey took me on our prearranged boat trip, permitting me to view the remainder of the island (see Figure 2).

The more I investigated the Oak Island enigma, the more skeptical I became. Others had preceded me in supplying what I came to regard as the two main pieces of the puzzle, although apparently no one had successfully fitted the pieces together. One concerned the nature of the "money pit" itself, the other the source of certain elements in the treasure saga, such as the reputed cryptogram-bearing stone.

Man-Made or Natural?

Doubts begin with the reported discovery in 1795 of the treasure shaft itself. While some accounts say that the trio of youths spied an old ship's pulley hanging from a branch over a depression in the ground (Harris 1958, 6–8), that is "likely an apocryphal detail added to the story later" and based on the assumption that some sort of lowering device

Figure 2. Offshore view of Oak Island showing site of Borehole 10X. The "Money Pit" lies just beyond.

would have been necessary in depositing the treasure (O'Connor 1988, 4). Nevertheless, some authors are remarkably specific about the features, one noting that the "old tackle block" was attached to "a large forked branch" of an oak "by means of a treenail connecting the fork in a small triangle" (Crooker 1978, 17). Another account (cited in Finnan 1997, 28) further claims there were "strange markings" carved on the tree. On the other hand, perhaps realizing that pirates or other treasure hoarders would have been unlikely to betray their secret work by leaving such an obvious indicator in place, some versions of the tale agree that the limb "had been sawed off" but that "the stump showed evidence of ropes and tackle" (Randle 1995, 75).

Similarly, the notion that there was a log platform at each ten-foot interval of the pit for a total of nine or eleven platforms, is only supported by *later* accounts, and those appear to have been derived by picking and choosing from earlier ones so as to create a composite version of the layers. For example, the account in the *Colonist* (1864) mentions that the original treasure hunters found only flagstones at two feet ("evidently not formed there by nature") and "a tier of oak logs" located "ten feet lower down" (i.e., at twelve feet). They continued some "fifteen feet farther down," whereupon—with no mention of anything further of note—they decided to stop until they could obtain assistance. James McNutt, who was a member of a group of treasure hunters working on Oak Island in 1863, described a different arrangement of layers (Crooker 1978, 24).

In 1911 an engineer, Captain Henry L. Bowdoin, who had done extensive borings on the island, concluded that the treasure was imaginary. He questioned the authenticity of various alleged findings (such as the cipher stone and piece of gold chain) and attributed the rest to natural phenomena (Bowdoin 1911). Subsequent skeptics have proposed that the legendary Money Pit was nothing more than a sinkhole caused by the ground settling over a void in the underlying rock (*Atlantic* 1965). The strata beneath Oak Island are basically limestone and anhydrite (Crooker 1978, 85; Blankenship 1999), which are associated with the formation of solution caverns and salt domes. The surface above caverns, as well as over faults and fissures, may be characterized by sinkholes.

Indeed, a sinkhole actually appeared on Oak Island in 1878. A woman named Sophia Sellers was plowing when the earth suddenly sank beneath her oxen. Ever afterward known as the "Cave-in Pit," it was located just over a hundred yards east of the Money Pit and directly above the "flood tunnel" (O'Connor 1988, 51).

Geologist E. Rudolph Faribault found "numerous" sinkholes on the mainland opposite Oak Island, and in a geological report of 1911 concluded there was "strong evidence" to indicate that the purported artificial structures on the island were "really but natural sink holes and cavities" (qtd. in Furneaux 1972). Further evidence of caverns in the area came in 1975 when a sewage-disposal system was being established on the mainland. Approximately 3,000 feet north of the island, workmen excavating with heavy machinery broke through a rock layer and discovered a 52-foot-deep cavern below (Crooker 1993, 144). Fred Nolan insists that in 1969, while drilling on Oak Island, Triton broke into a cavern near the fabled treasure shaft at a depth of 165 feet. "Blankenship and Tobias figured that the cavern was man-made," said Nolan, "but it isn't, as far as I'm concerned" (Crooker 1993, 165). And Mark Finnan (1997, 111), writing of "the unique geological nature of Oak Island," states as a fact that "naturally formed underground caverns are present in the island's bedrock." These would account for the flood "booby-traps" that were supposedly placed to guard the "treasure" (Preston 1988, 63).

Today, of course, after two centuries of excavation, the island's east end is "honey combed with shafts, tunnels and drill holes running in every imaginable direction" (Crooker 1978, 190), complicating the subterranean picture and making it difficult to determine the nature of the original pit. In suggesting that it was a sinkhole, caused by the slumping of debris in a fault, one writer noted that "this filling would be softer than the surrounding ground, and give the impression that it had been dug up before" (*Atlantic* 1965). Fallen trees could have sunk into the pit with its collapse, or "blowdowns" could periodically have washed into the depression (Preston 1988, 63), later giving the appearance of "platforms" of rotten logs.

Just such a pit was in fact discovered in 1949 on the shore of Mahone Bay, about five miles to the south of Oak Island, when workmen were digging a well. The particular site was chosen because the earth was rather soft there. Reports O'Connor (1988, 172–173): "At about two feet down a layer of fieldstone was struck. Then logs of spruce and oak were unearthed at irregular intervals, and some of the wood was charred. The immediate suspicion was that another Money Pit had been found."

The treasure seekers and mystery mongers are quick, however, to dismiss any thoughts that the "shaft" and "tunnels" could be nothing more than a sinkhole and natural channels. Why, the early accounts would then have to be "either gross exaggerations or outright lies," says one writer (O'Connor 1988, 173). For example, what about the reported "pick marks found in the walls of the pit" (O'Connor 1988, 173)? We have already seen—with the oak-limb-and-pulley detail—just how undependable are such story elements. Then what about the artifacts (such as the fragment of parchment) or the coconut fiber (often carried on ships as dunnage, used to protect cargo) found at various depths? Again, the sinkhole theory would explain how such items "worked their way into deep caverns under the island" (Preston 1988, 63).

Secrets Revealed

Assuming the "shaft" is a natural phenomenon, there still remains the other major piece of the Oak Island puzzle: How do we explain the presence of such cryptic elements as the cipher stone allegedly discovered in the pit in 1803, a large equilateral triangle (made of beach stones and measuring ten feet on each side) found in 1897, or a megalithic cross which Fred Nolan discovered on the south shore in 1981? (See Figure 1; Finnan 1997, 36, 68–69, 79–82.)

By the early 1980s I had become aware of parallels between Oak Island's Money Pit and the arcana of the Freemasons. Theirs is not, they insist, a "secret society" but a "society with secrets." Carried to North America in the eighteenth century, Masonry has been defined as "a peculiar system of morality veiled in allegory and illustrated by symbols" (*Masonic* 1964, 26). One of the essential elements of any true Masonic group is "a legend or allegory relating to the building of King Solomon's

Temple" ("Freemasonry" 1978). And an allegory of the Secret Vault, based on Solomon's fabled depository of certain great secrets, is elaborated in the seventh or Royal Arch degree. Among the ruins of the temple, three sojourners discover the subterranean chamber wherein are found three trying-squares and a chest, identified as the Ark of the Covenant (*Masonic* 1964, 12, 37, 63; Lester 1977, 150; Duncan 1972).

No doubt many readers have encountered Secret Vault symbolism—which pertains to lost secrets, buried treasure, and the grave (Macoy 1908, 445; *Revised* 1975, 64 n.22)—without recognizing it as such. For example, Sir Arthur Conan Doyle, a Freemason, not only employed Masonic allusions in several of his Sherlock Holmes stories (Bunson 1994, 84) but penned three that evoke Masonry's hidden vault itself. For instance, Holmes uncovers dark secrets in "The Adventure of Shoscombe Old Place." Beneath an old chapel on the Shoscombe property, accessed by stumbling through "loose masonry" (an obvious pun) and proceeding down a steep stairway, Holmes finds himself in a crypt with an "arched . . . roof" (evoking the Royal Arch degree of Masonry). Accompanied by his client—a "Mr. Mason"!—Holmes finds the key to a series of strange mysteries. Similarly allusive Holmes stories are "The Red-Headed League" (featuring a client who sports a Masonic breastpin), and the suggestively titled "The Musgrave Ritual."

In addition to the Sherlockian Secret Vault allegories there are several examples of the genre that many people have taken at face value, believing them true accounts. One, for example, is the tale of Swift's Lost Silver Mine of eastern Kentucky. In his alleged journal, one "Jonathan Swift" explored the region prior to Daniel Boone, marking a tree with "the symbols of a compasses, trowel and square"—Masonic emblems—and discovering and mining silver (which geologists doubt exists in the region). Leaving to seek backers, Swift says he stored the treasure in a cave and "walled it up with masonry form." Later he became blind and unable to find his fabled treasure (although still capable of writing in his journal!). This evokes Masonic ritual wherein a candidate must enter the lodge in *complete blindness* (i.e. blindfolded) to begin his quest for enlightenment (Nickell 1980).

Another such lost-treasure story is found in the purported Beale Papers, which tell a tale of adventure, unsolved ciphers, and fabulous treasure. This was "deposited" in a stone-lined "vault" (using language from the Select Masters' degree) in Virginia. The papers were published by a Freemason (Nickell 1982b).

Then there is the "restless coffins" enigma of the Chase Vault of

Barbados. According to proliferating but historically dubious accounts, each time the vault was opened, between 1812 and 1820, the coffins were discovered in a state of confusion. After they were reordered the vault was closed by "masons." Yet the coffins would again be found in disarray. At least two of the men involved were high-ranking Free-masons. In 1943 another restless-coffins case occurred on the island, this time specifically involving *a party of Freemasons* with the vault being that of *the founder of Freemasonry in Barbados!* (Nickell 1982a)

It now appears that another such tale is the legend of Oak Island, where again we find unmistakable evidence of Masonic involvement. There are, of course, the parallels between the Money Pit story and the Masonic Secret Vault allegory. The "strange markings" reportedly carved on the oak adjacent to the Pit suggest *Masons' Marks*, inscribed signs by which Masons are distinguished (Waite 1970, xx; Hunter 1996, 58). The three alleged discoverers of the Pit would seem to represent the *Three Worthy Sojourners* (with Daniel McInnis representing the *Principal Sojourner*), who discover the Secret Vault in the Royal Arch de-gree (Duncan 1972, 261). In that ritual the candidate is lowered on a rope through a succession of trap doors, not unlike the workmen who were on occasion hauled up and down the (allegedly platform-intersected) Oak Island shaft. The tools used by the latter—notably spades, pickax-es, and crowbar (O'Connor 1988, 2; Harris 1958, 15)—represent the three *Working Tools* of the Royal Arch Mason (Duncan 1972, 241). Indeed, when in 1803 workers probed the bottom of the Pit with a crowbar and struck what they thought was a treasure chest, their actions recall the Royal Arch degree in which the Secret Vault is located by a sounding blow from a crowbar (Duncan 1972, 263). The parallels go on and on. For example, the soft stone, charcoal, and clay found in the Pit (Crooker 1978, 24, 49) are consistent with the *Chalk, Charcoal and Clay* cited in the Masonic de-gree of Entered Apprentice as symbolizing the virtues of "freedom, fer-vency and zeal" (Lester 1977, 60; Hunter 1996, 37).

Then there are the artifacts. Of course many of these—like the old branding iron found in the swamp (Crooker 1993, 175, 176)—are prob-ably nothing more than relics of the early settlers. Some are actually suspicious, like the links of gold chain found in the Pit in 1849. One ac-count holds that they were planted by workers to inspire continued operations (O'Connor 1988, 177–178).

Other artifacts are more suggestive, like the cipher stone (again see Figure 1), which disappeared about 1919. Its text has allegedly been pre-served, albeit in various forms and decipherments (Rosenbaum 1973,

83). For instance zoologist-turned-epigrapher Barry Fell thought the inscription was ancient Coptic, its message urging people to remember God lest they perish (Finnan 1997, 148–149). In fact, the text as we have it has been correctly deciphered (and redeciphered by several investigators, me included). Written in what is known as a simple-substitution cipher, it reads, "Forty Feet Below Two Million Pounds Are Buried" (Crooker 1993, 23). Most Oak Island researchers consider the text a hoax (O'Connor 1988, 14), but as Crooker (1993, 24) observes, an inscribed stone *did* exist, "having been mentioned in all the early accounts of the Onslow company's expedition." Significantly, a cipher message (with key), found in the Secret Vault, is a central aspect of Freemasonry's Royal Arch degree (Duncan 1972, 248–249).

Other artifacts (Finnan 1997, 67, 80, 83) that appear to have ritualistic significance are the stone triangle and great "Christian Cross" as well as "a handworked heart-shaped stone"—Masonic symbols all. Crooker (1993, 179) notes that "a large amount of time and labor" were spent in laying out the cross, but to what end? Could it have been part of a Masonic ritual?

An "old metal set-square" found at Smith's Cove may simply be an innocent artifact, but we recall that three small squares were among the items found in the Secret Vault (Duncan 1972, 243). Indeed, the square is one of the major symbols of Freemasonry that, united with a pair of compasses, composes the universal Masonic emblem.

Explicitly Masonic, I believe, are certain inscribed stones on the island. These include one discovered at Joudrey's Cove by Gilbert Hedden in 1936. It features a *cross* flanked by the letter *H*, said to be a modification of the Hebraic letter for Jehovah, and a prime Masonic symbol known as a *Point Within a Circle*, representing mankind within the compass of God's creation (Morris n.d., 47; Finnan 1997, 66, 151). Another clearly Masonic stone is a granite boulder found near the Cave-in Pit in 1967. Overturned by a bulldozer, it bore on its underside the letter *G*, in a rectangle (what Masons term an *oblong square*). *G* denotes the Grand Geometer of the Universe—God, the central focus of Masonic teachings—and is "the most public and familiar of all symbols in Freemasonry," observes Mark Finnan (1997, 152). He continues: "The presence of this symbol on Oak Island and its location in the east, seen as the source of light in Masonic teachings, is further indication that individuals with a fundamental knowledge of Freemasonry were likely involved."

Indeed, the search for the Oak Island treasure "vault" has been carried out largely by prominent Nova Scotia Freemasons. I had an intimation of this years ago, but it fell to others, especially Finnan who gained access to Masonic records, to provide the evidence. Freemasonry had come to Nova Scotia in 1738 and, concludes Finnan (1997, 145), "it is almost a certainty that organizers of the first coordinated dig . . . were Masonicly associated." Moreover, he states: "Successive treasure hunts throughout the past two hundred years often involved men who were prominent members of Masonic lodges. Some had passed through the higher levels of initiation, and a few even held the highest office possible within the Fraternity."

They include A. O. Creighton, the Oak Island Association treasurer who helped remove the cipher-inscribed stone from the island about 1865, and Frederick Blair, whose family was involved in the quest as far back as 1863. Blair, who formed the Oak Island Treasure Company in 1893, was a "prominent member" of the lodge in Amherst, Nova Scotia. Treasure hunter William Chappell was another active Mason, and his son Mel served as Provincial Grand Master for Nova Scotia from 1944 to 1946 (Finnan 1997, 145–146). Furthermore, discovered Finnan (1997, 146):

> The independently wealthy Gilbert Hedden of Chatham, New Jersey, who carried out the treasure search from 1934 to 1938, and Professor Edwin Hamilton, who succeeded him and operated on the island for the next six years, were also Freemasons. Hamilton had at one time held the office of Grand Master of the Grand Lodge of Massachusetts. Hedden even made it his business to inform Mason King George VI of England about developments on Oak Island in 1939, and Hamilton corresponded with President [Franklin D.] Roosevelt, another famous Freemason directly associated with the mystery.

(Roosevelt actually participated in the work on Oak Island during the summer and fall of 1909.) Other Masonic notables involved in Oak Island were polar explorer Richard E. Byrd and actor John Wayne (Sora 1999, 12; Hamill and Gilbert 1998).

Significantly, Reginald Harris, who wrote the first comprehensive book on Oak Island at the behest of Frederick Blair, was an attorney for Blair and Hedden. Himself a thirty-third-degree Mason, Harris was provincial Grand Master from 1932 to 1935. Among his extensive papers were notes on Oak Island, scribbled on the backs of Masonic documents and sheets of Masonic letterhead. The papers show that at least one Oak Island business meeting was held in the Masonic Hall in Halifax, where Harris had an office as secretary of the Grand Lodge (O'Connor 1988, 93; Harris 1958, vii; Finnan 1997, 143; Rosenbaum 1973; 154).

One investigator, Ron Rosenbaum (1973, 154), discovered that among Harris's papers were "fragments of a Masonic pageant" that were apparently "designed to accompany the rite of initiation into the thirty-second degree of the Masonic Craft." The allegory is set in 1535 at the Abbey of Glastonsbury, where the Prime Minister is attempting to confiscate the order's fabulous treasures. But one item, the chalice used at the Last Supper—the Holy Grail itself—is missing, and secret Masons are suspected of having hidden it for safekeeping. The allegory breaks off with them being led to the Tower for torture.

Given this draft allegory by Harris, it may not be a coincidence that some recent writers attempt to link the Holy Grail to Oak Island. They speculate that the fabled chalice is among the lost treasures of the Knights Templar, precursors of the Freemasons (Sora 1999, 180, 247–251).

In any event, the evidence indicates a strong Masonic connection to the Oak Island enigma. Others have noted this link but unfortunately also believed in an actual treasure of some sort concealed in a man-made shaft or tunnel (Crooker 1993; Finnan 1997; Sora 1999; Rosenbaum 1973). Only by understanding both pieces of the puzzle and fitting them together correctly can the Oak Island mystery finally be solved.

In summary, therefore, I suggest first that the "Money Pit" and "pirate tunnels" are nothing of the sort but are instead natural formations. Secondly, I suggest that much of the Oak Island saga—certain reported actions and alleged discoveries—can best be understood in light of Freemasonry's Secret Vault allegory. Although it is difficult to know at this juncture whether the Masonic elements were opportunistically added to an existing treasure quest or whether the entire affair was a Masonic creation from the outset, I believe the mystery has been solved. The solution is perhaps an unusual one but no more so than the saga of Oak Island itself.

References

Atlantic Advocate. 1965. Article in October issue, cited in Crooker 1978, 85–86.

Blankenship, Dan. 1999. Author interview, July 1.

Bowdoin, H. L. 1911. Solving the mystery of Oak Island. Collier's Magazine, August 18. Cited and discussed in Harris 1958, 110–120; O'Connor 1988, 63–66.

Bunson, Matthew E. 1994. Encyclopedia Sherlockiana. New York: Barnes & Noble.

Colombo, John Robert. 1988. Mysterious Canada: Strange Sights, Extraordinary Events, and Peculiar Places. Toronto: Doubleday Canada Limited.

Crooker, William S. 1978. The Oak Island Quest. Hantsport, N.S.: Lancelot Press.

———. 1993. Oak Island Gold. Halifax, N.S.: Nimbus.

Duncan, Malcolm C. 1972. Duncan's Masonic Ritual and Monitor. Chicago: Ezra A. Cook, 217–265.

Finnan, Mark. 1997. Oak Island Secrets, rev. ed. Halifax, N.S.: Formac.

"Freemasonry." 1978. Collier's Encyclopedia.

Furneaux, Rupert. 1972. *The Money Pit Mystery*. New York: Dodd, Mead & Co.

Hamill, John, and Robert Gilbert. 1998. *Freemasonry*. North Dighton, Mass.: J. G. Press, 228, 241, 245.

Harris, R. V. 1958. *The Oak Island Mystery*. Toronto: Ryerson.

Hunter, C. Bruce. 1996. *Masonic Dictionary*, 3rd ed. Richmond, Va.: Macoy.

Lester, Ralph P. ed. 1977. *Look to the East!* rev. ed. Chicago: Ezra A. Cook.

Macoy, Robert. 1908. *Illustrated History and Cyclopedia of Freemasonry*. New York: Macoy.

Masonic Heirloom Edition Holy Bible. 1964. Wichita, Kansas: Heirloom Bible Publishers.

Morris, W. J. N.d. *Pocket Lexicon of Freemasonry*. Chicago: Ezra A. Cook.

Nickell, Joe. 1980. Uncovered—The fabulous silver mines of Swift and Filson, *Filson Club History Quarterly* 54 (October): 325–345.

———. 1982a. Barbados' restless coffins laid to rest. *Fate*, Part I, 35.4 (April): 50–56; Part II, 35.5 (May): 79–86.

———. 1982b. DISCOVERED: The secret of Beale's treasure, *Virginia Magazine of History and Biography* 90, no. 3 (July): 310–324.

———. 2000. Canada's mysterious maritimes. *Skeptical Inquirer* 24(1), January/February: 15–19.

O'Connor, D'Arcy. 1988. *The Big Dig*. New York: Ballantine.

Preston, Douglas. 1988. Death trap defies treasure seekers for two centuries. *The Smithsonian*. June, 53–63.

Randle, Kevin D. 1995. *Lost Gold & Buried Treasure*. New York: M. Evans and Co., 75–107.

Revised Knight Templarism Illustrated. 1975. Chicago: Ezra A. Cook.

Rosenbaum, Ron. 1973. The mystery of Oak Island. *Esquire* 79 (February): 77–85, 154–157.

Sora, Steven. 1999. *The Lost Treasure of the Knights Templar*. Rochester, Vermont: Destiny.

Waite, Arthur Edward. 1970. *A New Encyclopedia of Freemasonry*. New York: Weathervane.

Acknowledgments

I am indebted to many people for helping to make this book possible: CSI executive director Barry Karr for giving a green light; director of CFI Libraries, Tim Binga, for research assistance; Paul E. Loynes for typesetting; Julia Lavarnway for editing; and Chris Fix for art direction.

I am also grateful to James Randi, my mentor; Paul Kurtz, for setting me on the road to become a full-time, professional paranormal investigator; and John and Mary Frantz, whose generosity in establishing a fund for my exclusive use has made possible many of my investigations. I also want to acknowledge my late friends, Steve Allen and Robert A. Baker, who—along with my parents—I miss every day but whose encouragement and guidance are remembered whenever I think of them.

Many others deserve special mention: Vaughn Rees and Martin Mahner, who have traveled extensively with me; Tom Flynn for expertise in many areas, including videography; ditto John F. Fischer for his forensic assistance; and many, many others, notably CFI's CEO Ronald Lindsey, *Skeptical Inquirer* editor Kendrick Frazier, the entire CFI staff for their continued support, and the many colleagues around the world who have generously offered their assistance and encouragement—among them Massimo Polidoro, Luigi Garlaschelli, Jan Willem Nienhuys, and many others.

Finally, I am grateful to my family—my wife, Diana Gawen Harris; daughter, Cherie Roycroft; and grandchildren, Chase, Tyner, and Alexis Jo—who fill every day with love.

Select Annotated Bibliography

Baker, Robert A. *Hidden Memories: Voices and Visions from Within*. Buffalo, N.Y.: Prometheus Books, 1992. A noted psychologist's discussion of such phenomena as alien abductions, past-life regression, spirit communication, and the like—exploring faulty memory, hypnosis, hallucinations, and other illusions and delusions.

Baker, Robert A., and Joe Nickell. *Missing Pieces: How to Investigate Ghosts, UFOs, Psychics, and Other Mysteries*. Buffalo, N.Y.: Prometheus Books, 1992. An investigative manual containing rules of evidence, investigative tactics, case synopses, and other fundamentals for the paranormal investigator.

Binder, David A., and Paul Bergman. *Fact Investigation: From Hypothesis to Proof*. St. Paul: West, 1984. Legally oriented treatment of the gathering and evaluation of evidence, formulation of hypotheses, etc.

Christopher, Milbourne. *ESP, Seers & Psychics: What the Occult Really Is*. New York: Thomas Y. Crowell, 1970. A penetrating skeptical look at the world of the "occult," including penetrating analyses of spiritualism, ghosts, and psychic phenomena.

Gardner, Martin. *Fads and Fallacies in the Name of Science*. New York: Dover, 1957. A great skeptics' classic with penetrating insights into pseudoscientific theories, cults, and cranks; essential reading.

Hines, Terence. *Pseudoscience and the Paranormal: A Critical Examination of the Evidence*. Amherst, N.Y.: Prometheus Books, 1988. A psychologist's look at the evidence behind such claims as alien abductions, biorhythms, graphology, and the like.

Houdini, Harry. *A Magician Among the Spirits*. New York: Harper & Brothers, 1924. A master magician's exposé of fraudulent mediums during the heyday of spiritualism.

Houp, Kenneth W., Thomas E. Pearsall, and Elizabeth Tebeaux. *Reporting Technical Information*, eighth ed. Boston: Allyn and Bacon, 1995. An excellent technical-writing textbook.

Keene, M. Lamar. *The Psychic Mafia*. Amherst, N.Y.: Prometheus Books, 1997. As told to Allen Spraggett, a confessed charlatan's account of his former life as a fraudulent spiritualist medium, revealing secrets of the practice.

Klass, Philip J. *UFOs Explained*. New York: Vintage Books, 1974. Introduction to flying-saucer reports by a major critical examiner of claims of extraterrestrial visitations.

Kurtz, Paul. *The Transcendental Temptation: A Critique of Religion and the Paranormal*. Buffalo, N.Y.: Prometheus Books, 1986. A critical analysis of the bases of religion, drawing parallels between today's paranormal beliefs and the religions of the past.

———. *Exuberant Skepticism*, ed. by John R. Shook. Amherst, N.Y.: Prometheus Books,

2010. A bible for the modern skeptical movement, eschewing mere debunking for "skeptical inquiry" and a positive outlook.

Kurtz, Paul, ed. *A Skeptic's Handbook of Parapsychology.* Buffalo, N.Y.: Prometheus Books, 1985. A critical examination of parapsychological claims by noted experts.

————, ed. *Skeptical Odysseys: Personal Accounts by the World's Leading Paranormal Inquirers.* Amherst, N.Y.: Prometheus Books, 2001. Reflections by critical inquirers into claims of the paranormal, with many autobiographical accounts.

Nickell, Joe. *The Magic Detectives: Join Them in Solving Strange Mysteries!* Amherst, N.Y.: Prometheus Books, 1989. A book inviting young readers to solve real paranormal cases using clues embedded in the text of each narrative.

————. *Looking for a Miracle: Weeping Icons, Relics, Stigmata, Visions & Healing Cures.* Amherst, N.Y.: Prometheus Books, 1993. A wide-ranging investigative study of phenomena held to be miraculous.

————. *Real-Life X-Files.* Lexington, Ky.: University Press of Kentucky, 2001. One of the author's casebooks of his paranormal investigations—along with *Secrets of the Supernatural* (1988), *The Mystery Chronicles* (2004), and *Adventures in Paranormal Investigation* (2007).

Nickell, Joe, with John F. Fischer. *Secrets of the Supernatural: Investigating the World's Occult Mysteries.* Amherst, N.Y.: Prometheus Books, 1999. Introductory textbook on forensics, with a true-crime case illuminating each topic.

Rachleff, Owen S. *The Occult Conceit: A New Look at Astrology, Witchcraft & Sorcery.* Chicago: Cowles Book Co., 1971. A highly readable, critical look at Ouija boards, witchcraft, and other occult interests.

Randi, James. *Flim-Flam! Psychics, ESP, Unicorns and Other Delusions.* Buffalo, N.Y.: Prometheus Books, 1982. A take-no-prisoners approach to paranormal and supernatural investigations, from an author known to magicians as The Amazing Randi.

————. *The Faith Healers.* Buffalo, N.Y.: Prometheus Books, 1987. Foreword by Carl Sagan. An exposé of faith-healing charlatans who claim to channel divine power to heal the sick but who actually trade false hope for cash.

————. *The Supernatural A-Z: The Truth and the Lies.* London: Brockhampton Press, 1995. Foreword by Arthur C. Clarke. A critical assessment of 666 allegedly supernatural topics, from *Abaris* (a Scythian magician) to *Zombie*.

Scot, Reginald. *The Discoverie of Witchcraft.* 1584; reprint of 1930 ed., New York: Dover, 1972. A surprisingly modern discrediting of the black arts by a witness to the witch-hunting mania.

Shermer, Michael. *Why People Believe Weird Things: Pseudoscience, Superstition, and Other Confusions of Our Time,* revised and expanded. New York: Henry Holt and Co., 2002. Introduction to critical thinking and antidote to conspiracy theories and other irrationalities such as belief in "scientific creationism."

Stein, Gordon. *Encyclopedia of Hoaxes.* Detroit: Gale Research, 1993. Foreword by Martin Gardner. Wide-ranging examination of famous hoaxes, such as the Cardiff Giant, Amityville Horror, Piltdown Man, Cottingley Fairies, Shroud of Turin, Jersey Devil, and many, many more.